Doll Dress
BOUTIQUE

SEW 40+ PROJECTS FOR 18" DOLLS

a dress for every occasion

ERIN HENTZEL

C&T PUBLISHING

PUBLISHER: Amy Marson

CREATIVE DIRECTOR: Gailen Runge

ACQUISITIONS EDITOR: Roxane Cerda

MANAGING EDITOR: Liz Aneloski

EDITOR: Katie Van Amburg

TECHNICAL EDITOR: Alison M. Schmidt

COVER/BOOK DESIGNER: April Mostek

PRODUCTION COORDINATOR: Tim Manibusan

PRODUCTION EDITOR: Jennifer Warren

ILLUSTRATOR: Linda Johnson

PHOTO ASSISTANT: Mai Yong Vang

STYLE PHOTOGRAPHY by Lucy Glover and INSTRUCTIONAL PHOTOGRAPHY by Mai Yong Vang of C&T Publishing, Inc., unless otherwise noted

Published by C&T Publishing, Inc., P.O. Box 1456, Lafayette, CA 94549

Library of Congress Cataloging-in-Publication Data

Names: Hentzel, Erin, 1966- author.

Title: Doll dress boutique : sew 40+ projects for 18˝ dolls : a dress for every occasion / Erin Hentzel.

Description: Lafayette, CA : C&T Publishing, Inc., 2018. | Includes bibliographical references.

Identifiers: LCCN 2017061190 | ISBN 9781617456695 (soft cover)

Subjects: LCSH: Doll clothes--Patterns.

Classification: LCC TT175.7 .H466 2018 | DDC 745.592/21--dc23

LC record available at https://lccn.loc.gov/2017061190

Printed in China

10 9 8 7 6 5 4

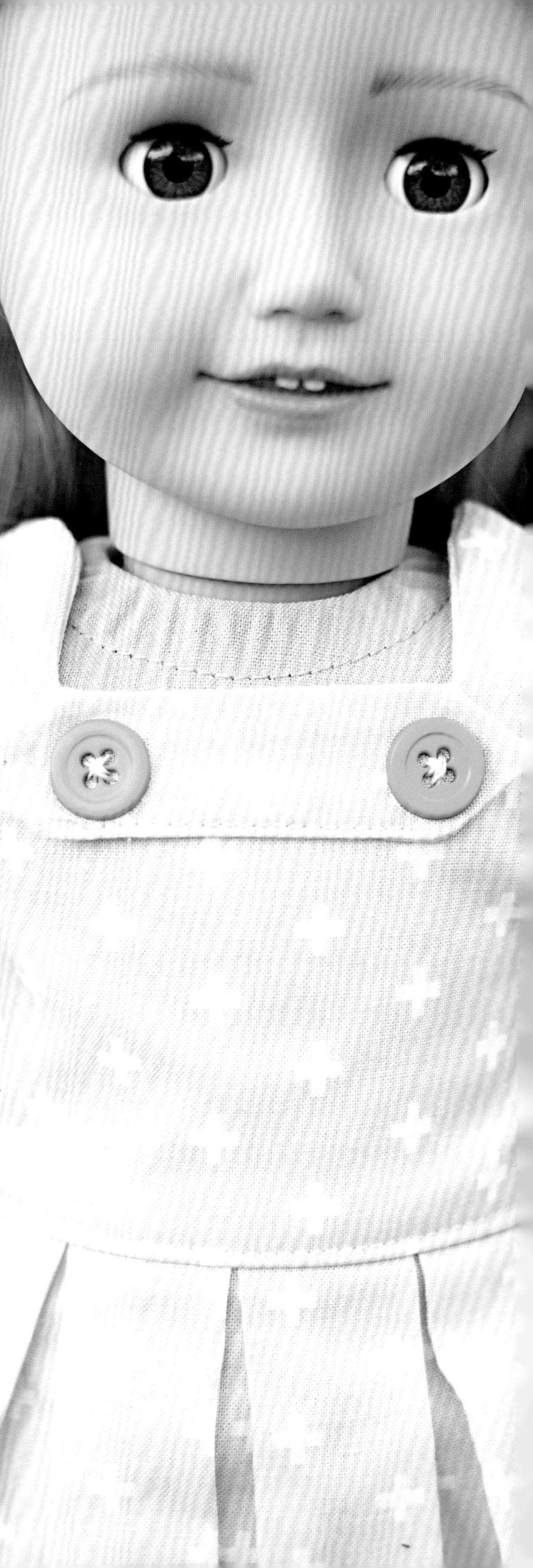

Dedication

This book is dedicated to all doll dressmakers, young and not so young alike. I hope you love sewing these dresses as much as I loved creating them. May this book help you to keep your dolls—or the dolls of your daughters, granddaughters, nieces, and loved ones—all impeccably dressed.

Acknowledgments

A warm, heartfelt thanks to my husband, who has always believed in me, and to my children, for their patience, encouragement, and love.

My sincere thanks to the following individuals and companies:

My students, whose enthusiasm for sewing makes me smile and inspires me to keep creating. It's such a privilege to be a part of your sewing journey.

My friend Bee (who sells her wares in her Etsy shop, A Bee Line), for using her wonderful cobbler skills to make several matching pairs of shoes for me to use in my book.

Roxane, Liz, Gailen, Katie, Alison, Lucy, Mai, April, Linda, Jennifer, and everyone at C&T whose talent, expertise, and hard work helped make my book amazing and beautiful.

Dear Stella, Riley Blake Designs, and Timeless Treasures Fabrics, for providing me with gorgeous fabric with which to create many of these cute doll dresses.

C&T Publishing, for giving me the opportunity to create this book.

Contents

WELCOME
ABOARD

FOREWORD

A FEW THOUGHTS ABOUT DESIGNING FOR DOLLS

Design it well. Choose high-quality fabric, add delicate details, and keep a consistent scale. Complete each step carefully and to the best of your ability, and your designs will get noticed.

Choose fabric that is appropriate for the design, has a soft hand, drapes well, and has an appropriate print scale. Always center any distinct motif onto the bodice front, especially with larger-scale prints. Matching plaids and stripes when possible helps take your sewing to a higher level of excellence.

Simplicity is the keynote of all true elegance.

—Coco Chanel

Don't underestimate the power of a simple, classic look; styles that stand the test of time do so for a reason. Choose a gorgeous fabric and allow the design to speak for itself. Understanding color and its effects on a design will empower you to utilize color in many ways—such as creating mood, optical illusions, and emphasis—transforming the ordinary into the extraordinary.

According to *The Vogue Sewing Book*, trims are the mark of a creative seamstress. Paying special attention to detail enables you to elevate your sewing to the next level. A doll dress can have great details, setting it apart from other designs. When looking for lace and trims, choose micro trims that will maintain the scale, giving your doll dress both harmony and balance.

Fit matters. The fit not only affects the overall look of a dress but also things like its drape and silhouette line. Try the dress on your doll as you sew. This will help you make any adjustments to the dress to fit your doll.

The fabric choice affects the fit. It's best to use finer, lightweight quilting cottons. Avoid thicker, rough-feeling quilting cottons—they add bulk to each seam and may cause a fit issue. These fabrics will negatively affect the lines and drape of a design. Instead, look for soft-feeling cottons with a higher thread count. In other words, use a higher-quality fabric to achieve a better-looking dress.

You can't use up creativity. The more you use, the more you have.

—Maya Angelou

You are a creative artist each time you sew. Interview the trims and fabrics as you plan your doll dress. Oftentimes, I end up with two or three dress ideas during the interview process. This process can be fun—take your time choosing! After all, it's this creative process that brings us our love of sewing.

—Erin

Introduction

This book is written for the doll dressmaker who has made many doll dresses and has a firm understanding of sewing basics, such as gathering, sewing center back closures, and finishing seam allowances. This is not a book for learning the basics—rather, it is a doll clothes pattern book. However, I invite you to join my Facebook sewing group, where you can ask sewing questions and get help sewing these patterns (see About the Author, page 63).

Many of the sewing techniques are repeated in one or more dresses within *Doll Dress Boutique*. Instead of repeating the same instructions within each project, the detailed instructions are provided in Chapter One: General Sewing (page 8), and a page reference is given within the project instructions.

After sewing a few dresses with the same construction techniques, you may not need to refer to the tutorials as often, especially as you become a seasoned doll dressmaker. This structure enables you as the dressmaker to mix and match design elements with ease.

Suggested Fabrics

Lightweight woven cotton is ideal for making doll dresses (including the lining). Fabrics such as quilting cotton, oxford cloth, seersucker, lawn, poplin, piqué, chambray, and linen fabric will work well for our purposes.

Thread Choice

Be sure the thread you choose blends in or matches well with the fabric. Otherwise the thread may stand out in a negative way. If you want the topstitching detail to be highlighted, choose a complementary or contrasting thread that coordinates well with the fabric.

Sewing Levels

Advanced beginner

Intermediate

Advanced

Patterns

The dolls shown in this book have a 10¾˝ chest and 10½˝ waist. The dresses are designed for the popular brand of 18˝ dolls, but the more fitted designs may not fit the older versions of these dolls.

The patterns are printed on both sides of the pullout sheet, so you will need to make a new copy, either by tracing or photocopying. For those who prefer to print and cut out their patterns, you can download them here:

tinyurl.com/11307-patterns-download

tip

Using Freezer Paper

Printer-friendly sheets of freezer paper (such as Quilter's Freezer Paper Sheets by C&T Publishing) are a game changer!

Patterns can be printed directly onto freezer paper using the download link provided.

Print (or trace) the patterns onto freezer-paper sheets. Iron the freezer paper, waxy side down, directly onto the fabric; cut out the pattern pieces; and peel the freezer paper off the fabric. These freezer-paper patterns can be used several times and won't leave any residue on the fabric.

Though you can print and cut out the patterns, I still recommend tracing them to prevent unnecessary wear on your fabric scissors.

Use Pellon 830 Easy Pattern or Swedish tracing paper to trace the patterns. The tracings will enable you to be more accurate when cutting out the fabric pieces and to fussy cut like a rock star. These pattern tracings can last a lot longer than paper patterns.

CHAPTER ONE

General Sewing

Finish the seam allowances of any exposed seam by sewing the raw edges with a zigzag or overcast stitch, using either a traditional sewing machine or a serger. You can also trim the raw edges of the fabric with pinking shears.

Pressing as you sew is extremely important. Make sure not to skip it! Press when instructed, and the results will be much more professional looking. An unpressed dress won't have the same lines or fit.

Tools in the Sewing Room

As a seasoned sewist, I'm sure you know your way around the notions aisle and have become best mates with your seam ripper. Here are some of my favorite tools that I use almost every time I sew a doll dress.

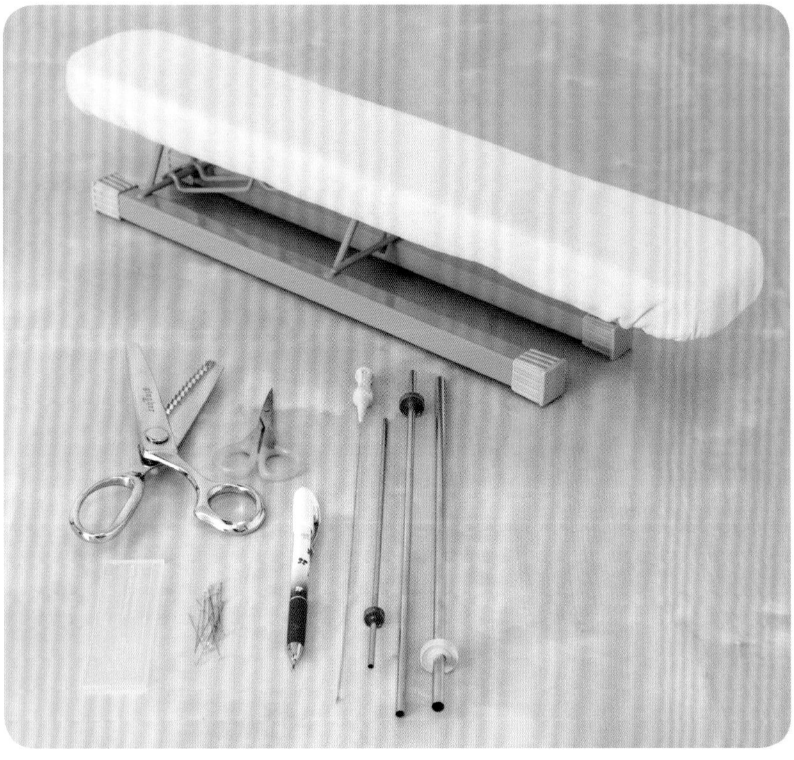

Superfine glass-head pins: Ultrafine or superfine pins are sharp and won't snag the fabric—perfect for pinning together the small pieces, especially those tricky sleeves or princess seams.

Sewline fabric marking pencil: This mechanical pencil marks accurately, and the markings are easily removed with a dab of water.

Small, sharp scissors: These are ideal for cutting little threads close to the fabric and clipping to the apex on collars and bodices, such as in Square-Neck Dresses (page 43).

2 × 4 Mighty Mini Board (by Clover): Little bodices fit perfectly over this ironing board.

Perfect Piecing Seam Guide ruler (by Perkins Dry Goods): Use this ruler to adjust the needle position for an accurate ¼″ seam allowance.

Pinking shears: Trim, finish, and cut notches in curved seam allowances—all in one step!

Fasturn: Quickly turn mini fabric pieces right side out and make spaghetti straps with ease.

Alex Anderson's 4-in-1 Essential Sewing Tool (by C&T Publishing): This other helpful turning tool is great for the shorter and wider pieces, such as collars and bows. It also contains a seam ripper, stiletto, and presser.

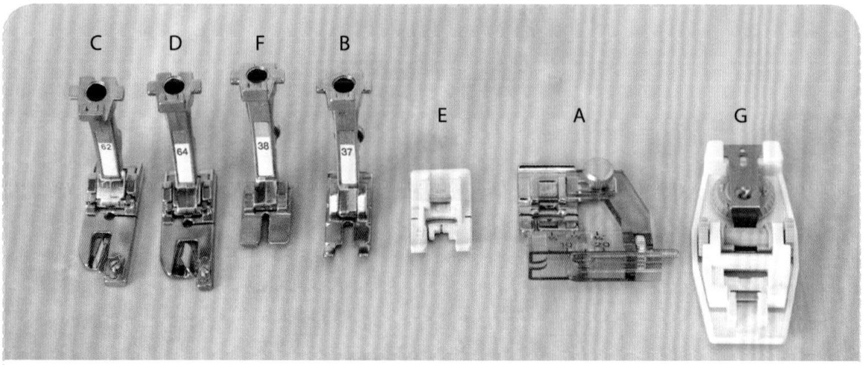

Specialty Presser Feet

Adjustable binding foot (A): This sews binding strips perfectly in one step.

¼˝ piecing foot (B): Sew with the edge of the foot even with the raw edge of the fabric pieces for ¼˝ seams.

Rolled narrow hem feet (C and D): Use these to create petite hems effortlessly and in no time at all. They are available in a variety of sizes, including 2 mm (C) and 4 mm (D), depending on your machine.

Nonstick/glide foot (E): A nonstick or glide foot slides easily over any fabric. It's perfect for sewing knits, elastic, and trims.

Piping foot (F): This foot takes the guesswork out of where to sew when adding piping trims.

Elastic foot (G): You can automatically stretch and sew elastic directly to the fabric with this foot.

tip

Clipping triangle-shaped notches in the seam allowances of a curved seam helps the seam spread and curve nicely. Use pinking shears to trim the seam allowances and quickly clip curved seams.

When sewing a seam with pivot points, such as the seams on the square and sweetheart necklines, trim away most of the seam allowance up to each pivot point in the seam. Grade the seam allowance along the sides leading up to the pivot point.

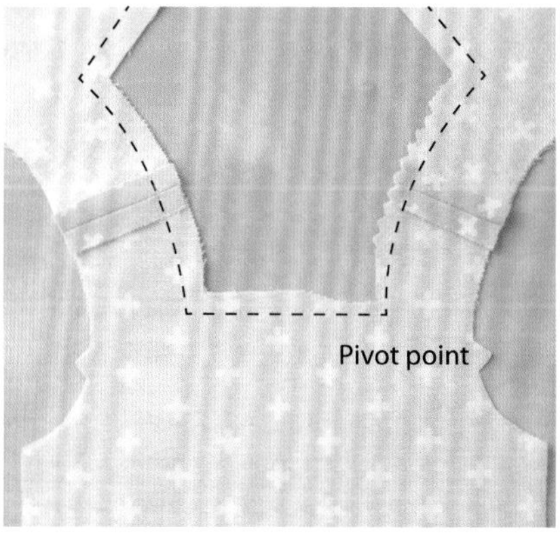

This also works well for the special collars on the Absolutely A-Line Dresses (page 22).

Sewing Bodices

Sew a Lined Bodice with Sleeves

1. Sew the bodice front to the bodice back at the shoulders, right sides together.

2. Press the seam allowances open.

3. If the design has an optional collar, baste it to the right side of the bodice.

4. Repeat Steps 1 and 2 for the lining.

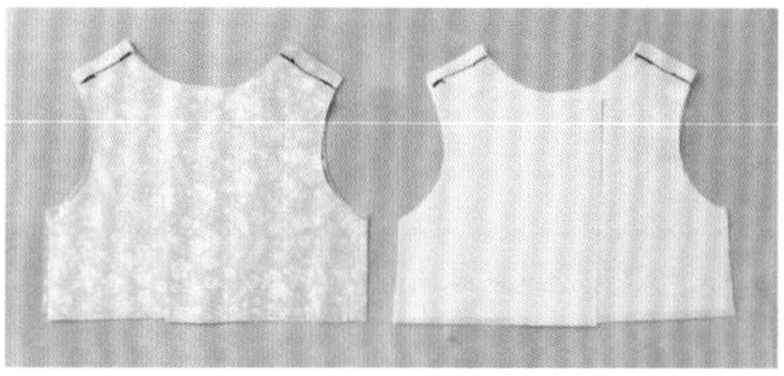

5. Sew the lining to the bodice at the neck edge, right sides together, and clip the curved seam allowances.

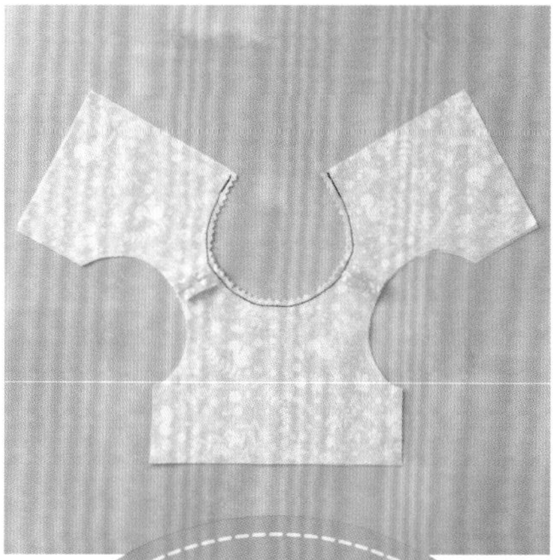

6. Separate the lining and bodice layers. Press the seam allowances toward the lining.

7. For regular round-neck bodices, understitch the lining—sewing also through the seam allowances—as close to the seam as possible around the entire neckline. *Note:* When adding a collar, be sure not to understitch the collar.

tip

Understitching ensures that the lining stays to the inside of the garment and helps hide the neckline seam for a neat and professional finish.

8. Fold the lining onto the main fabric with wrong sides together. Press well, aligning the raw edges.

9. Baste together the bodice and lining at the raw edges.

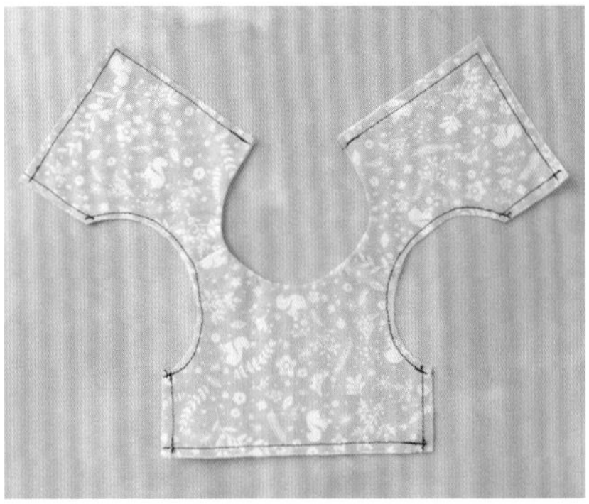

10. Topstitch the neckline. *Note:* Special-occasion fabrics such as silk, satin, and taffeta should not be topstitched.

Sew a Lined Bodice Without Sleeves

1. Follow Sew a Lined Bodice with Sleeves, Steps 1–5 (page 9). *Note:* If a collar has been added to the bodice, fold it toward the neckline and out of the path of the seam allowance before continuing.

2. Pin and sew the arm opening edge, right sides together.

3. Clip triangle notches in the curved seam allowances.

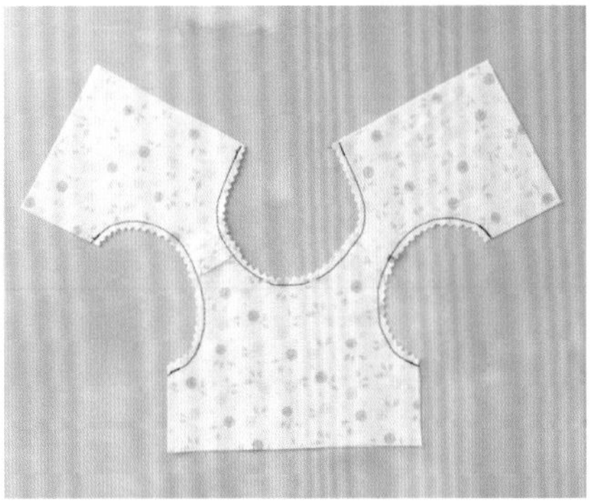

TURN THE BODICE

1. Pin a safety pin onto the lower edge of a back lining piece. Feed it through the shoulder tunnel until it comes out the bodice front side of the shoulder tunnel.

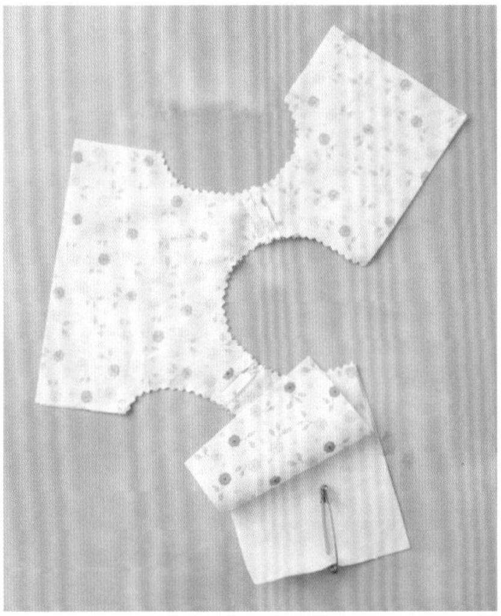

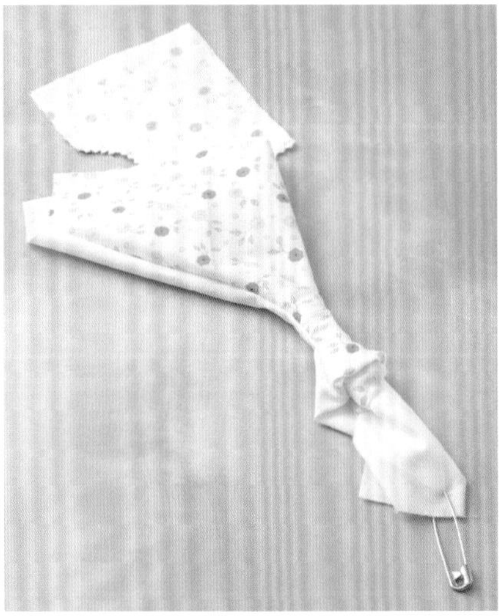

2. Gently pull the fabric right side out.

3. Repeat for the other side, turning through the other shoulder seam. Press the bodice.

4. Press open the seam allowances of the underarm seams just enough to easily sew the side seams.

SEW THE SIDE SEAMS

1. Pin and sew the bodice front to the bodice back and the lining front to the lining back at the sides, right sides together.

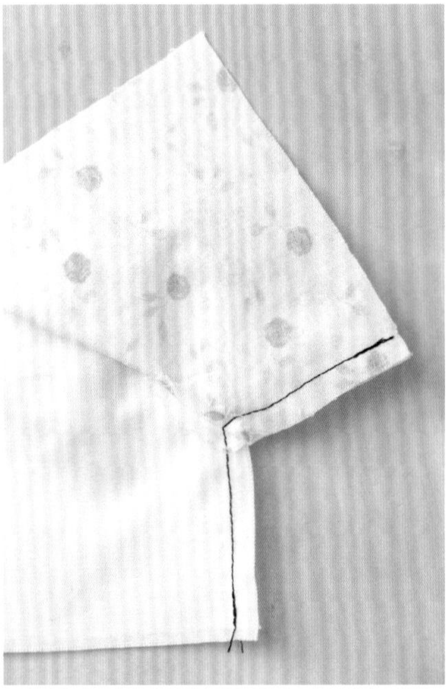

2. Press the seam allowances open and fold the bodice wrong sides together. Press.

3. Baste the center back and lower edge.

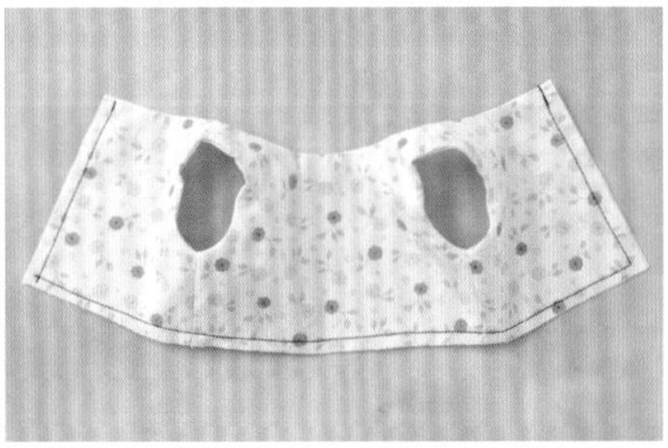

Sew a Bodice with Flutter or Half-Cap Sleeves

1. Follow Sew a Lined Bodice with Sleeves, Steps 1–5 (page 9).

2. Sew the flutter or half-cap sleeves to the right side of the bodice.

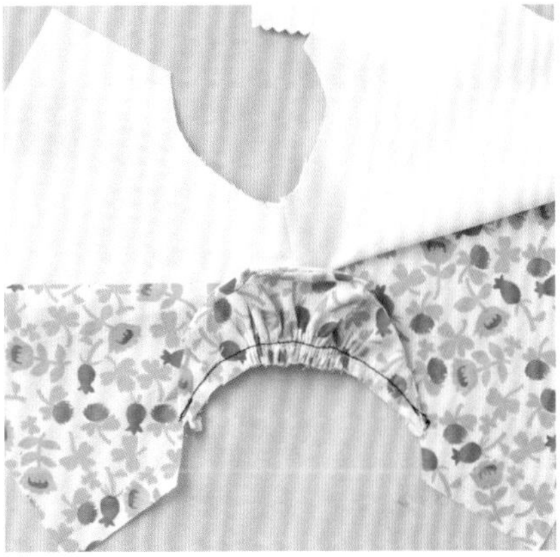

3. Continue to sew the lined bodice as if it were a bodice *without* sleeves: Starting with Sew a Lined Bodice Without Sleeves, Step 2 (previous page), sew the arm opening edges. *Note:* When sewing the arm opening edges, keep the sleeve ends folded and out of the way of the seam allowance.

Finishes

Finish with Bias Binding

This is a great technique to finish the openings on a garment, such as necklines and sleeve hems. A bias binding can also add a contrasting design element and give your design a little something special.

MAKE THE BIAS BINDING

Make sure to cut bias strips right on the bias (at a 45° angle from the grainline) so it curves more easily with the neckline or arm opening.

1. Cut out fabric strip(s) on the bias according to the project cutting instructions.

2. Fold each strip in half lengthwise, wrong sides together, and press.

3. Open up each strip and fold both raw edges to the center crease. Press.

4. Refold each strip in half lengthwise and press well.

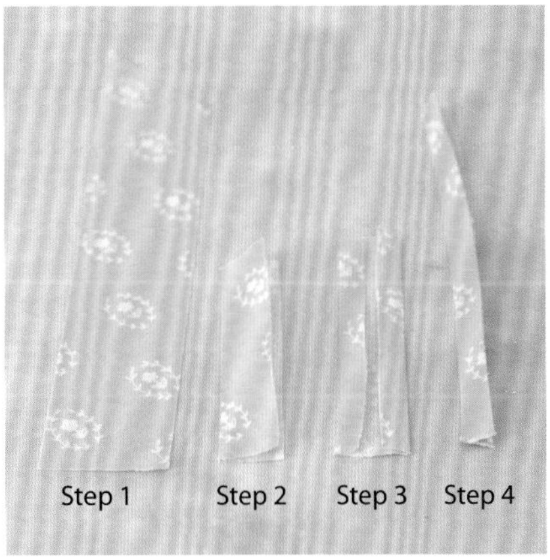

SEW THE BINDING TO THE GARMENT

1. Pin and sew the right side of the unfolded bias binding to the wrong side of the garment.

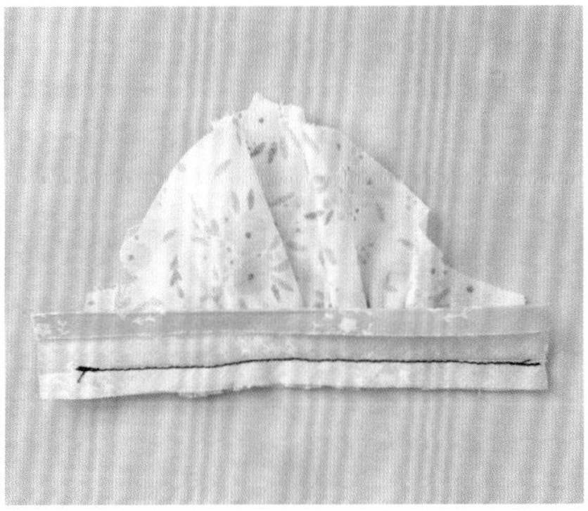

2. Fold the bias binding over to the right side of the garment. With the raw edge folded under, press the edge in place. If the edge is curved, such as in a neckline, shape the bias binding as you press, matching the curve.

3. Working with the right side facing up, sew the binding neatly in place, close to the folded edge.

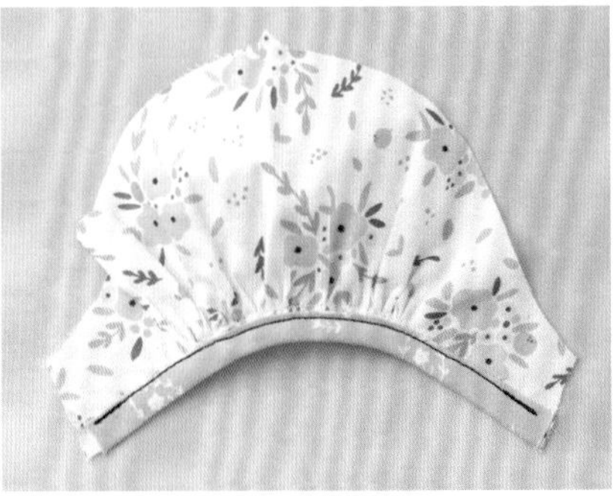

tip

If it's too bulky to easily fold the binding to the front and completely enclose the seam allowances, then trim the seam allowances slightly.

Hemming

DOUBLE-FOLDED HEM

The double-folded hem is a very neat finish, as no raw edges remain exposed.

Fold the fabric twice toward the wrong side of the fabric, pressing after each fold. Sew straight stitches across the folded fabric.

A ⅜˝ hem allowance is included in all the pattern pieces, so each fold should be slightly less than ¼˝ for a narrow hem. Using a rolled-hem presser foot works well for this type of hem.

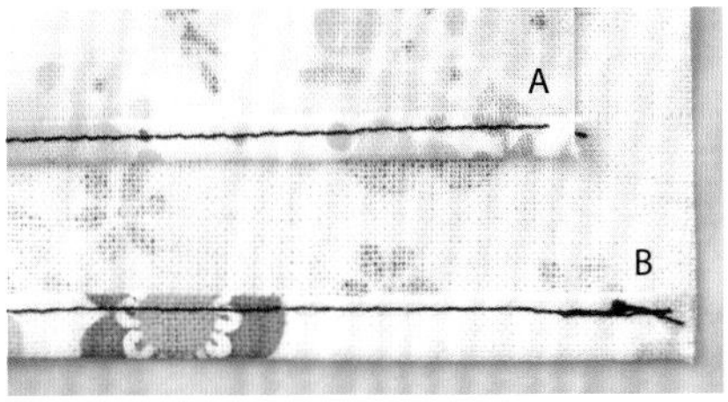

A. Sewn with ¼˝ rolled-hem presser foot
B. Sewn traditionally by folding twice, pressing after each fold, and sewing

SINGLE-FOLDED HEM

A single fold is more suitable for doll clothes, as it is less bulky than a double-folded hem. This quicker method makes hemming curved edges easy to manage.

1. Use a serger or an overcast stitch to finish the raw edge of the fabric.

2. Fold and press the fabric 3/8˝ to the wrong side. Sew the folded edge.

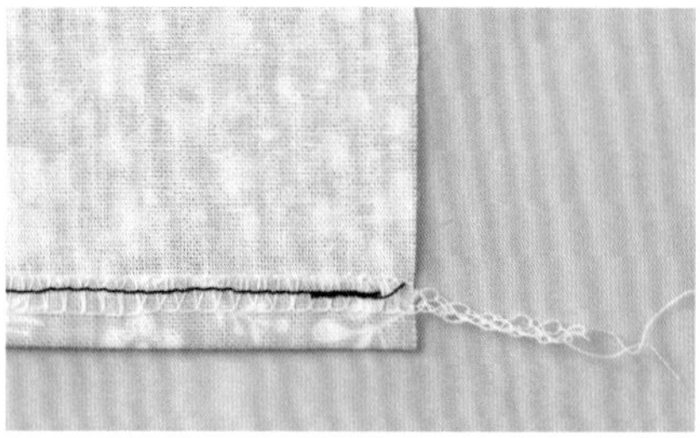

BINDING THE HEM

Using bias binding tape is a quick way to add drama to any dress.

Follow Finish with Bias Binding (page 11), or use a binding presser foot to do it all in one fast step.

HEMMING WITH TRIM

Hemming with trim works brilliantly with a rounded edge. Using purchased trim (such as lace) makes this a quick technique that gives any dress that *wow* factor.

1. Pin and sew the trim to the skirt piece, right sides together and placing the trim upside down.

2. Finish the raw edges.

3. Fold and press to the wrong side. Topstitch.

tip

When adding trim that is finished (such as cluny lace, edging trim, or rickrack), finish the raw edge of the skirt fabric before sewing the trim to it.

SEWING A CONTRAST HEM

1. Fold the contrast piece in half lengthwise, wrong sides together, and press.

tip

Pin and sew the trim to the contrast hem piece, keeping all raw edges even. This little detail adds a nice pop of color.

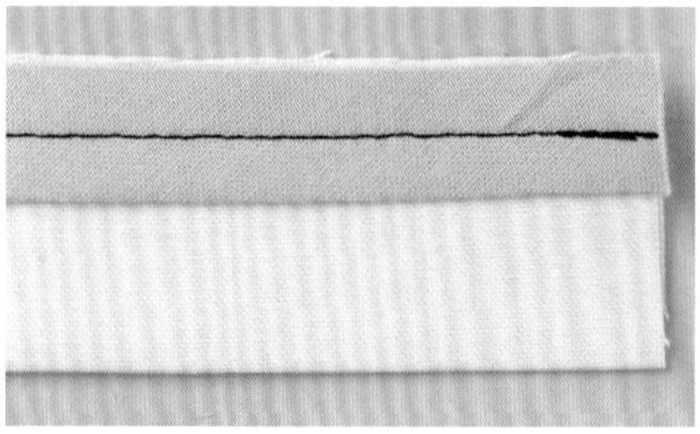

2. Pin and sew the contrast piece to the skirt piece, right sides together and using a 3/8˝ seam allowance.

3. Finish the seam allowances. Press them up toward the skirt piece.

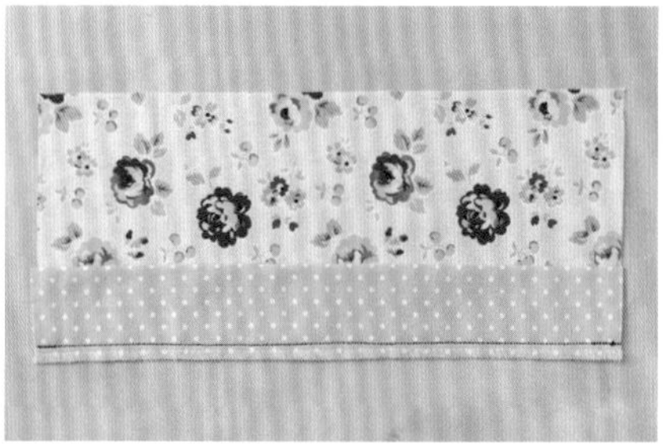

4. Topstitch along the skirt-piece side of the seam.

Elastic Finishes

CASING TECHNIQUES

Ideally, the casing should be just slightly wider than the width of the elastic so that the elastic fits snugly inside. Not only does this look best but this also prevents the elastic from twisting and turning inside the casing. You can use a double-fold or single-fold method to create a casing for elastic.

Single-Fold Method

1. Use a serger to simultaneously trim ¼˝ and overcast the raw edge.

2. Fold and press the fabric ⅜˝ to the wrong side. Sew straight stitches along the folded fabric, creating a casing at least ¼˝ wide.

Double-Fold Method

1. Fold and press the raw edge ¼˝ to the wrong side of the fabric.

2. Fold and press again ⅜˝ to the wrong side of the fabric.

3. Sew straight stitches along the folded fabric, creating a casing at least ¼˝ wide.

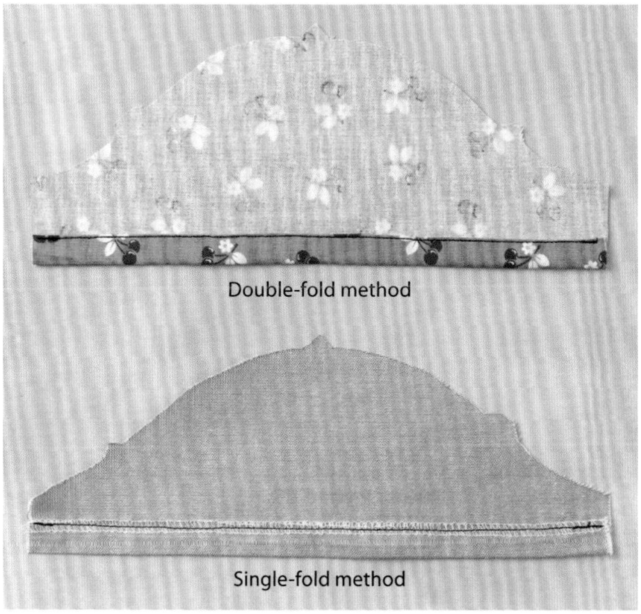

Inserting Elastic into the Casing

1. Place a safety pin on each end of the elastic and insert the elastic into the casing. When the tail end reaches the opening, remove the safety pin and sew across the width of the elastic to secure.

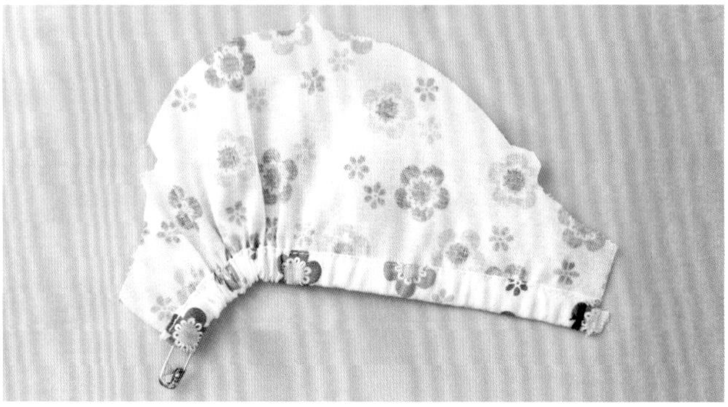

2. Continue to work the safety pin through until it comes out the other opening in the casing. Sew across the width to secure.

ELASTIC SEWN DIRECTLY TO THE FABRIC

1. Finish the edge of the garment with a narrow hem.

2. Pin the ends of the elastic piece to the edge of the sleeves.

3. Using a zigzag stitch, sew the elastic to the wrong side of the fabric ¼˝ from the finished edge, stretching the elastic as you sew it in place.

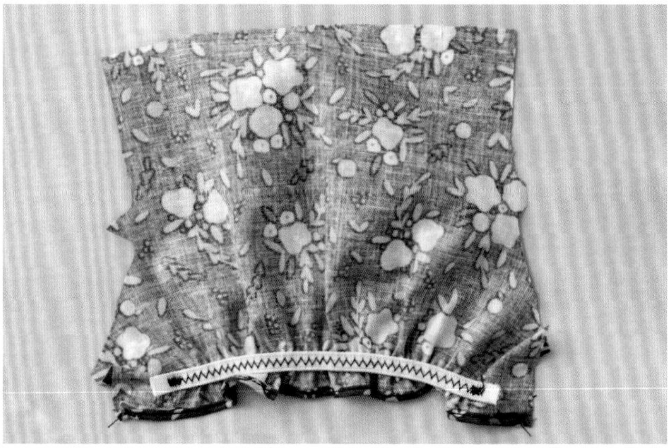

Skirts

Gathered Skirts

A lot of dresses get their twirl factor from gathered skirts. There are many ways to gather fabric; the most common way is to sew two parallel rows of long straight stitches and pull the bobbin threads at the same time.

tips

Sew the gathering stitches at ¼˝ and ½˝ from the raw edge, and sew the seam at ⅜˝. This makes it easy to remove the gathering stitches after sewing the seam.

- *Start and stop sewing the gathering stitches for the skirt 1˝ away from the center back opening edges.*
- *Anchor the gathering threads by wrapping them around a pin placed at the start of the gathering stitches. This allows the gathers to be distributed all the way to the 1˝ point. Make sure to remove the pin and move the gathering threads out of the way of the seam so you can still easily remove the gathering stitches once you've sewn the seam.*
- *To prevent the presser foot from pushing the gathers as you sew the gathered skirt to the bodice, reduce the presser foot pressure by half.*

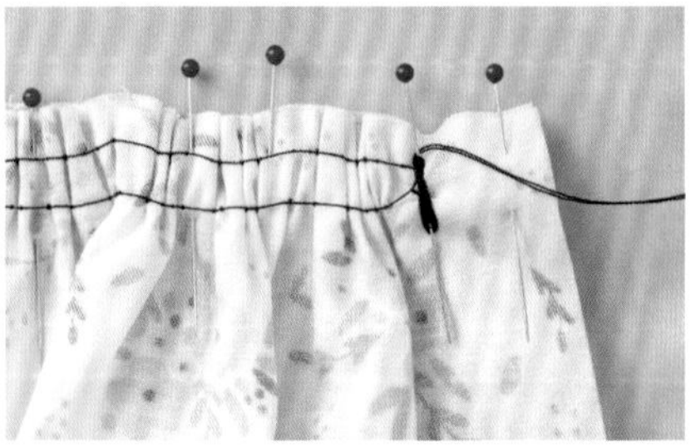

1. Pin and sew the gathered skirt to the bodice, right sides together and using a ⅜˝ seam allowance.

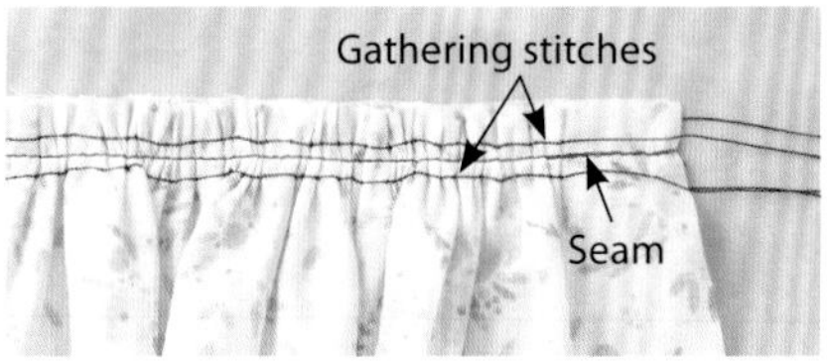

2. Finish the seam allowances. Press them toward the bodice or waistband.

3. Topstitch the lower edge of the bodice.

tip

If you have a serger, you can use it to quickly gather the skirt pieces, even if your machine does not have a differential feed feature.

1. *Serge the raw edge to be gathered using a 4- or 3-thread overcast. If available on your machine, set the differential feed to the gathering setting.*

2. *Pull on the needle thread(s) to gather and slide the gathers, distributing the gathers evenly.* Note: *The needle threads are the shorter threads in the serged thread chain.*

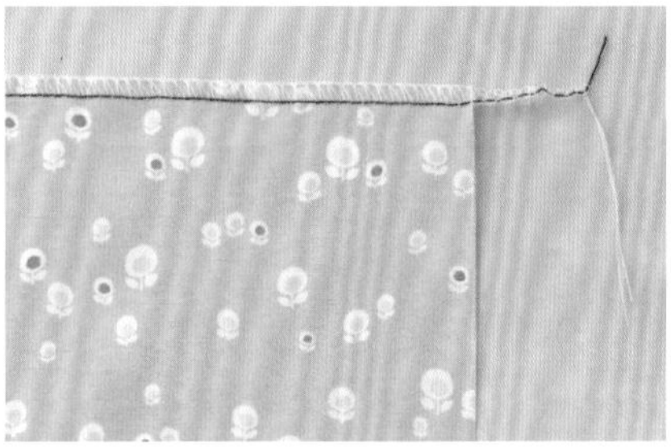

Three-thread overcast without differential feed, sewn to show thread position with dark thread in the needle and white thread in the loopers

Pull the needle thread(s) to gather the fabric.

Sew a Pleated Skirt

Mark the skirt fabric all along the upper edge with your choice of the pleat patterns shown (next page), starting 2˝ from the center back edge. There are three pleat markings on these patterns: the fold line, the placement line, and the direction in which the folded fabric should move.

MARKING PLEAT PATTERNS

Knife Pleats

Knife pleats move all the pleats in the same direction.

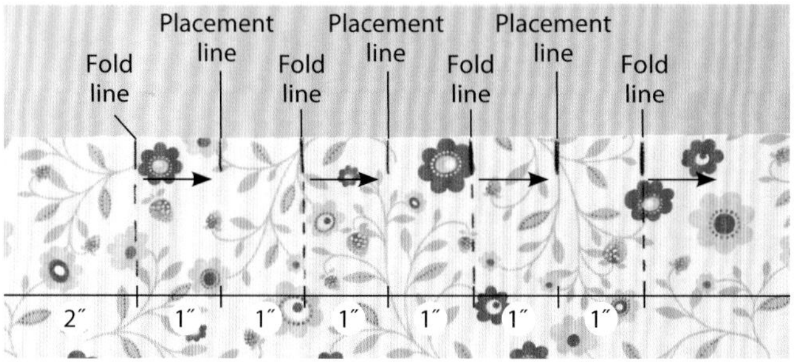

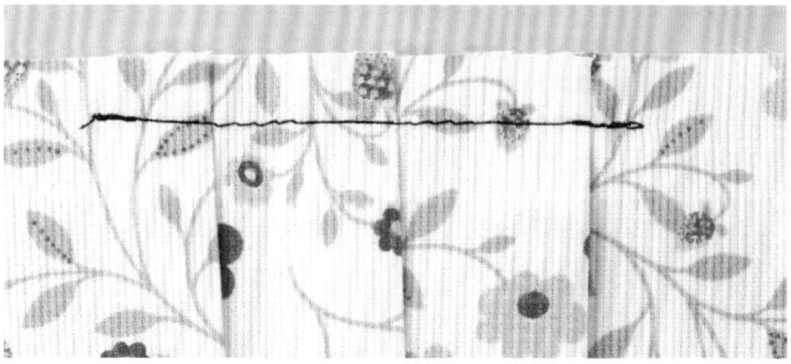

Knife pleats can also be placed closer together.

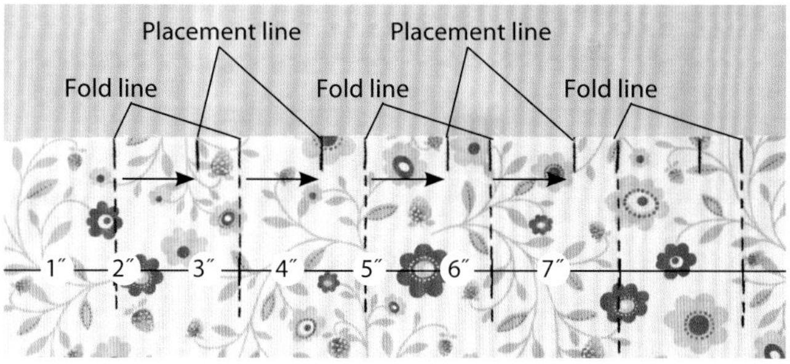

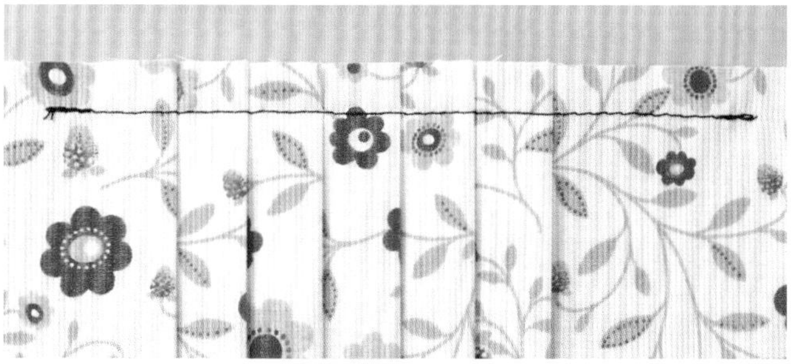

Inverted Box Pleats

Inverted box pleats move two pleats to a center point.

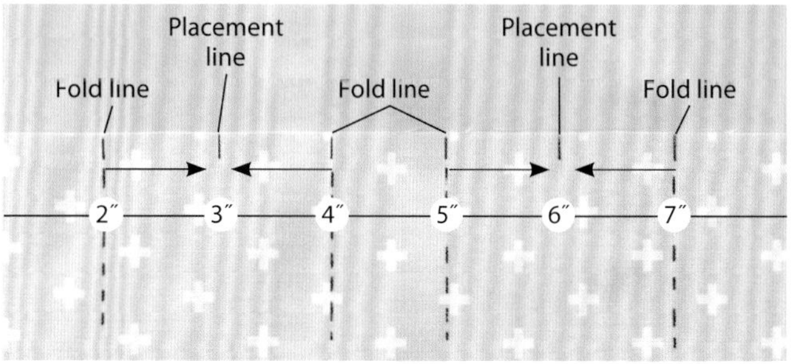

Inverted box-pleat design pattern for Sunny Day and Cape Cod (page 44)

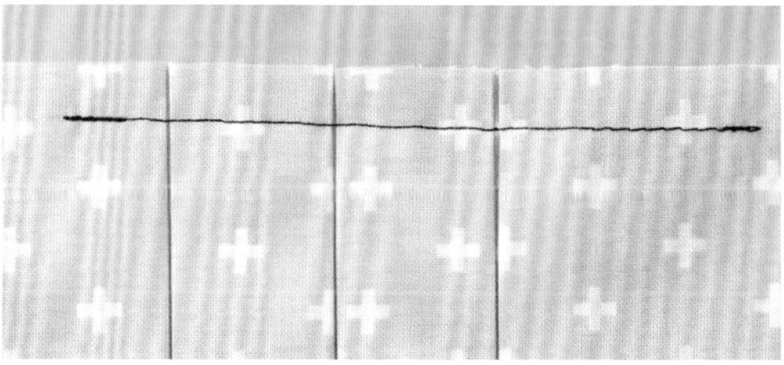

MAKING PLEATS

1. Fold the fabric with wrong sides together. Press sharply at the fold line, keeping the raw edges at the upper edge even.

2. Place the crease of the fold on the placement line.

3. After pressing all the pleats, baste them in place or sew the length of the fold to create tucks and growth pleats.

tip

Use painter's tape to hold the pleats in place after you have pressed and pinned.

Sew a Double-Layered Skirt

There are many ways to sew a double-layered skirt. The following is a quick, straightforward method. This skirt works best with lightweight fabrics, as the layers add bulk and cause the bodice to fit more tightly at the waist.

1. Hem both skirt pieces.

2. Place the overskirt on top of the underskirt so that both are facing right side up.

3. Treating the 2 skirts as a single piece of fabric, pin and sew 3 rows of gathering stitches along the upper edge of the skirt pieces, sewing through both layers of fabric.

4. Follow Gathered Skirts, Steps 1–3 (page 14).

Center Back Seam and Closures

You can sew the center back seam before or after sewing the hem. The particular design you choose will dictate the order.

Center Back Seam

1. Finish the raw edges of the center back.

2. Pin and sew the center back edge, right sides together and using a ½˝ seam allowance, from the hem to about 2˝–3˝ below the waist seam. Sewing too close to the waist makes putting the dress on the doll more challenging.

Sewing Center Back Closures

The ½˝ seam allowance of the center back opening can accommodate many types of closures, such as hook-and-loop tape, snaps, buttons, and zippers. Choose the closure that you prefer.

HOOK-AND-LOOP TAPE

tips

The all-in-one type of hook-and-loop tape is the ideal choice for doll clothes. It's double-sided, with one side being the hook side and the other being the loop side. It's ultrathin and doesn't add much bulk, making for a better-looking dress.

- *Another option is the soft and flexible type of hook-and-loop tape. It's less bulky than traditional hook-and-loop tape.*
- *If you use traditional hook-and-loop tape, trim it narrower to reduce the bulk in the back of the garment. I also recommend trimming the scratchy side of the hook-and-loop tape narrower than the soft side. This helps to prevent the doll's hair from getting caught in the tape, which can damage the hair.*

1. Press the seam allowances of the center back seam to one side. Continue to press *one side only* of the center back opening ½˝ to the wrong side so that one edge of the center back opening is folded and the other unfolded.

2. Cut the hook-and-loop tape to fit the opening.

3. Sew the scratchy side of the hook-and-loop tape to the *right* side of the fabric on the *unfolded edge* of the center back so that it will face away from the doll's body.

4. Sew the soft side of the hook-and-loop tape to the inside of the garment along the folded edge of the center back.

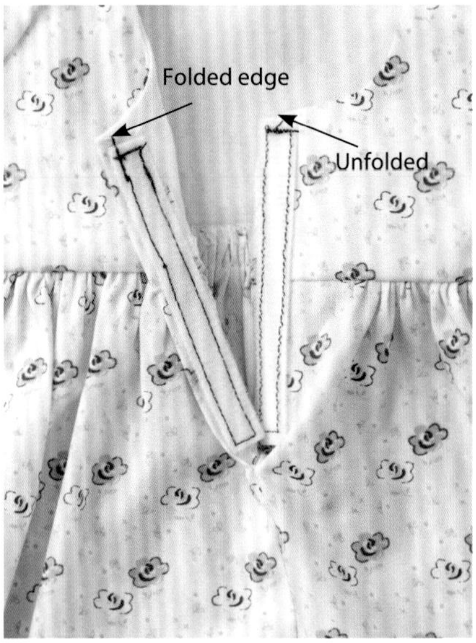

SNAPS

Snap pliers make adding snaps a snap! These pliers and colorful resin snaps are readily available and completely appropriate for doll clothes. Sew the center back seam and press to one side, just as when adding hook-and-loop tape. For best results, reinforce the center back edges with a scrap of fabric and/or interfacing.

BUTTONHOLES AND BUTTONS

Most machines have an automatic buttonhole capability that makes creating buttonholes effortless. Following your sewing machine manual's instructions, practice on some scrap fabric—you may find buttonholes much easier than you anticipated!

Sew the center back seam and press to one side, just as when adding hook-and-loop tape. Prepare the fabric and center back opening for buttons and buttonholes.

1. Fuse fusible interfacing onto the wrong side of the fabric on both edges of the center back opening.

2. Mark the buttonhole placements at least ¼˝ from the folded edge of the center back opening. Follow your sewing machine manual to make the buttonholes.

3. Place straight pins at both bar tacks of the buttonhole. Open up the buttonholes using a seam ripper or small, sharp scissors.

4. Sew buttons to the unfolded edge of the center back opening.

You can create other types of buttonholes for an easier method, like using ribbons to make loop-style buttonholes. The result can be quite pretty!

Creative Details

Sew a Collar or Yoke

1. Pin and sew together the yoke or collar pieces, right sides together, leaving the neck edge unsewn.

2. Clip the curves and corners. Turn right side out and use a corner-turning tool to gently poke out the corners. Press.

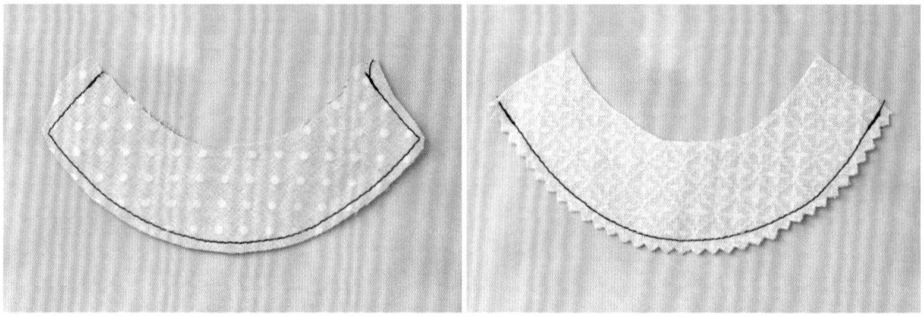

For Princess-Seamed Dresses (page 55), only sew the yoke's lower edge.

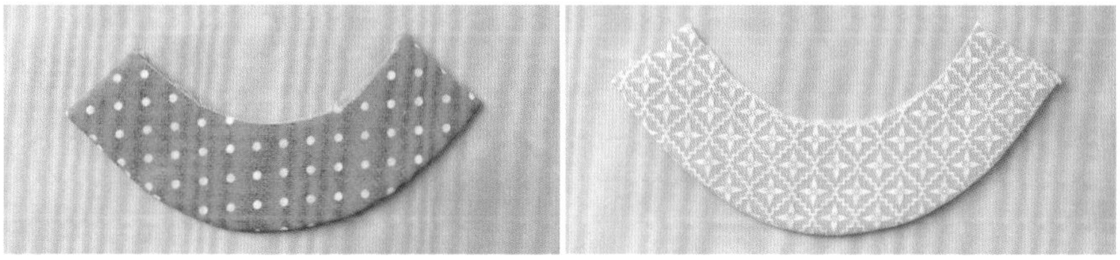

3. Pin and sew the collar(s) or yoke to the right side of the bodice, keeping the shoulder and/or neck edges even.

Sew the collar(s) to the bodice after sewing the shoulder seams and before sewing it to the lining.

Sew the yoke to the bodice before sewing the shoulder seams.

Make a Fabric Sash

A fabric sash adds a sweet touch to any dress, creating rhythm and emphasis. You can simply tie a sash on the dress or sew it in place at the sides for a more permanent design feature. If you're sewing the sash in place, it's easier to sew it to the dress before sewing the center back seam.

1. Cut a sash piece from fabric according to the project instructions, or use these measurements:

Gathered sash: 2¼˝ × 34˝

Simple sash: 1½˝ × 34˝

2. Sew narrow hems on both long edges. *(Watch as I demonstrate this technique in a video: youtube.com/user/candtpublishing > search How to Sew Petite Hems for Doll Dresses.)*

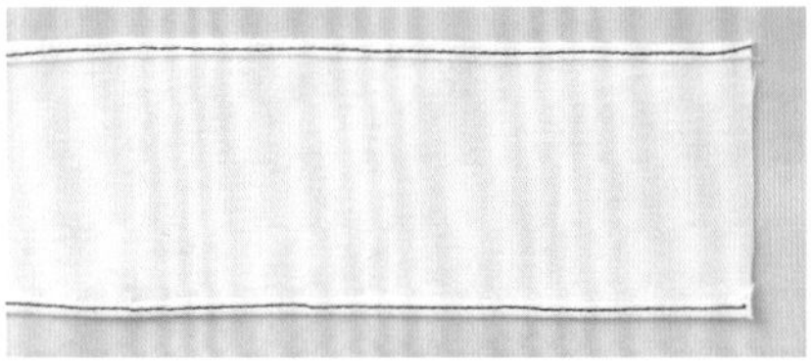

3. Finish the raw edges of the short ends.

4. Fold and press the short ends ¼˝ to the wrong side.

5. Sew the folded edge.

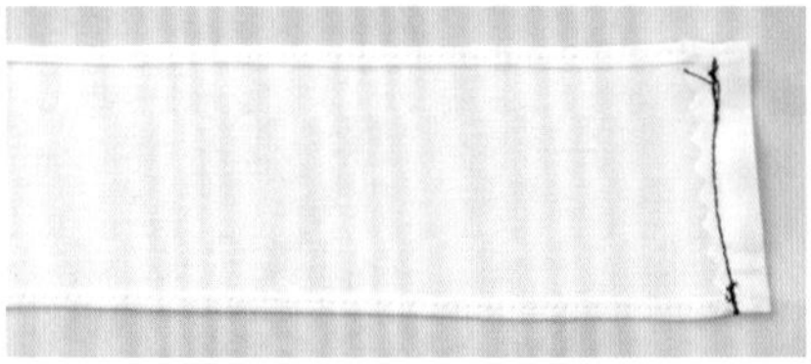

6. *Optional:* To create a pointed tip, fold the end again into a 45° angle. Sew across the side edge to secure it in place.

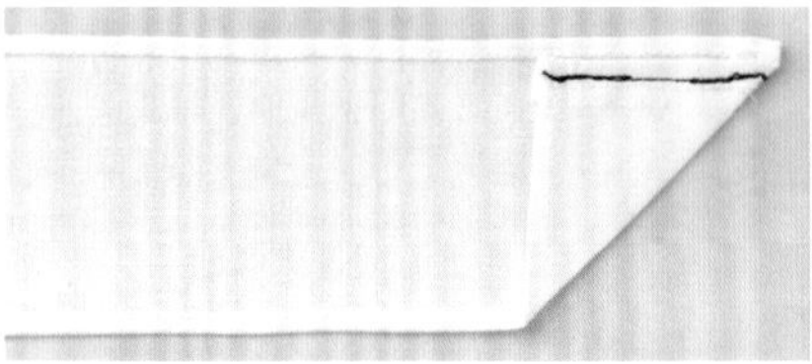

GATHERED SASH

1. Tie the sash onto the waist of the dress and mark the points at which the sash meets the side seams.

2. Sew gathering stitches on the sash where marked in Step 1. Gather it to approximately 1˝.

3. Pin and sew the sash in place at the side seams. Remove the gathering stitches.

Make a Ruffle

You can add a ruffle to a neckline, sleeve, or hemline.

1. Cut a ruffle as directed in the project cutting instructions.

2. Hem one long edge.

tip

When creating rolled hems with a serger, be sure to use the rolled-hem setting. It looks much more polished than the standard overlock stitch. Use wooly nylon thread in the loopers to create a more decorative hem.

3. Sew gathering stitches along the opposite long edge.

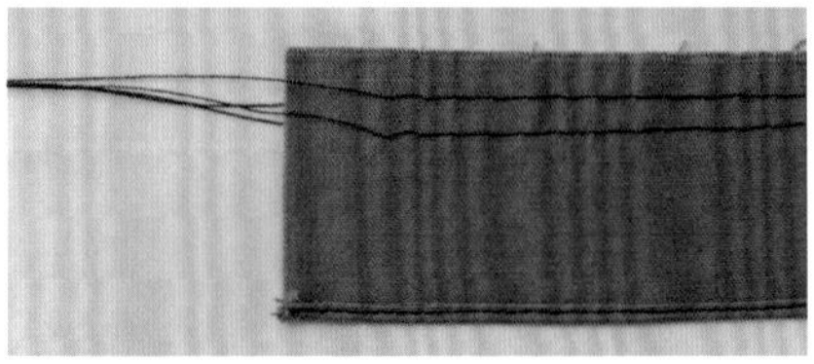

4. Pull on the bobbin threads to gather the ruffle to fit the dress.

SEWING THE RUFFLE TO A SKIRT OR SLEEVE

1. Gather the ruffle to fit the skirt piece or sleeve end.

2. Pin and sew the ruffle to the skirt or sleeve, right sides together and using a ⅜˝ seam allowance.

3. Finish the seam allowances. Press them toward the skirt or sleeve.

4. Topstitch on the skirt or sleeve side of the pressed seam.

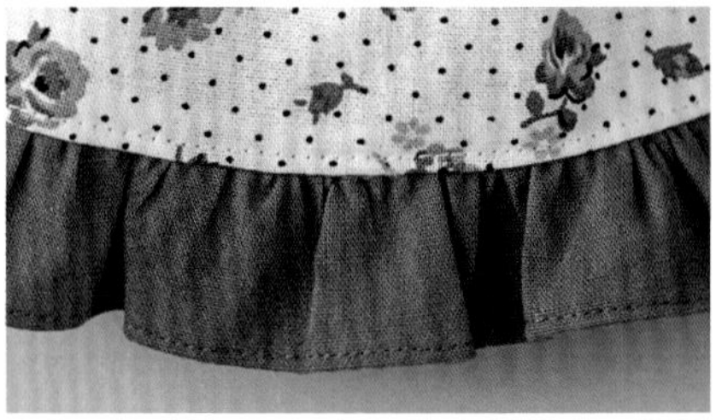

RUFFLE DETAIL

1. Hem both long edges of the fabric strip.

2. Sew a row of gathering stitches down the center.

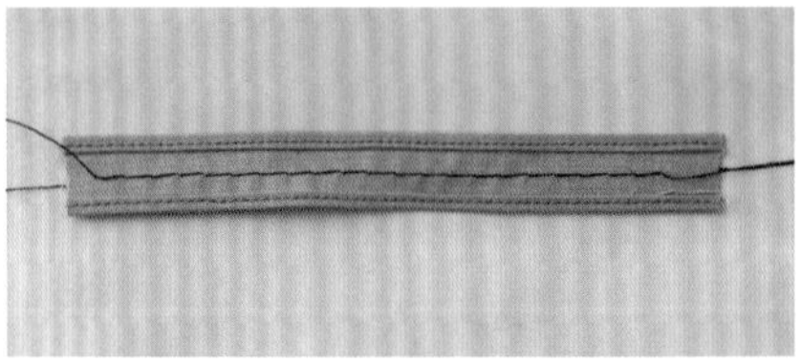

3. Gather the ruffle. Fold the short ends to the wrong side, and sew the ruffle onto the right side of the garment, with the right side of the ruffle facing up.

Tuxedo Twirl

Create a ruffle detail that finishes at 1⅜″ × 5½″. Gather the ruffle detail to fit the bodice, and sew it to a lined bodice before sewing the bodice to the skirt piece. Add buttons and a classic bow to finish the mock placket.

Use the Bodice Front 13, Bodice Back 14, and Skirt Piece 23 (short length) patterns, adding ¼″ to the center back edges of the skirt piece to accommodate the wider bodices of the Classic Sleeveless Dresses (page 29).

Make a Bow

FABRIC BOW

These bows are *tiny*, so it's easiest to tie them when using lightweight fabrics. You can use this technique to make the bodice embellishment piece for the Sunny Day dress (page 44) and the belt for the Blomstring dress (page 57).

1. Use the Bow 10 pattern to cut out the fabric pieces.

2. Using a short stitch length, pin and sew the bow pieces with right sides together. Leave an opening where indicated on the pattern.

tip

If you don't have a Fasturn tool, you can sew ribbon into the bow pieces to quickly turn them right side out. Use cheap satin ribbon because it frays and is removed easily.

1. *Cut the ribbon piece(s) longer than the piece to be turned. Cut 2 pieces for the bow and 1 piece for the belt.*

2. *Sew the ribbon(s) into the end(s) when sewing together the bow and belt pieces.*

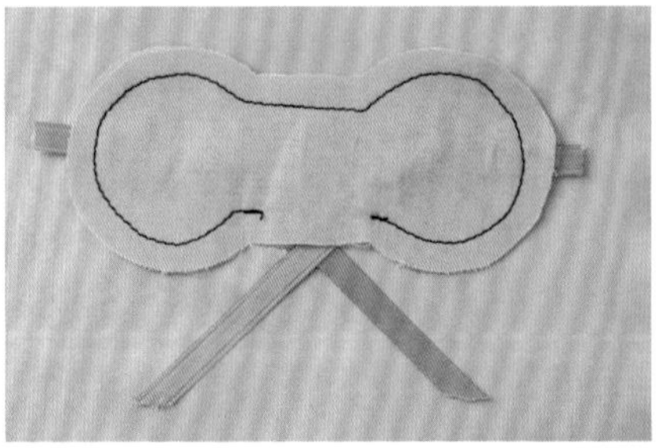

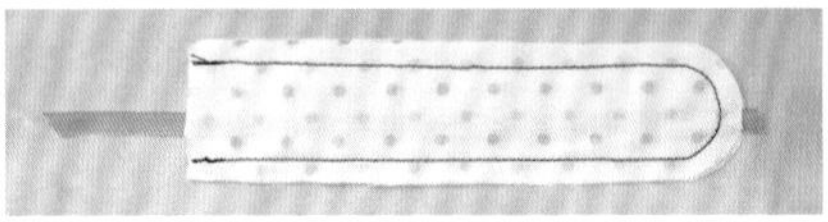

3. *Pull on the ribbon(s) to turn the piece right side out.*

4. *After the piece has been turned right side out, cut the ribbon(s) close to the fabric and pull any leftover remnants of the ribbon(s).*

3. Clip the curves and turn right side out with a Fasturn tool.

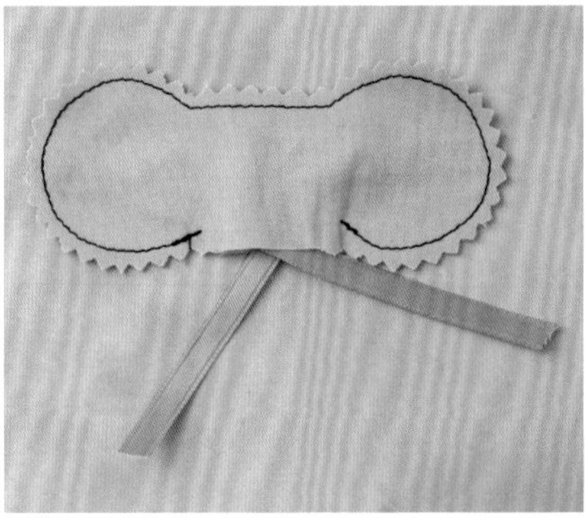

Use a corner-turning tool like the pointed wood end cap in Alex Anderson's 4-in-1 Essential Sewing Tool or a wooden knitting needle to smooth out the rounded edges. Press. Use the nose of the iron to push the fabric and create the round edges.

4. Press the raw edges of the opening to the inside. Sew the opening closed.

5. Tie the bow piece into a knot at the center and hand sew it onto the yoke, bodice, or waist of the dress. *Note:* The bow is very small and may be difficult to tie into a knot. Wrap it around a knitting needle, instead of a finger, to make tying it easier.

CLASSIC BOW

1. Use the Classic Bow 11 and 12 patterns to cut out the fabric pieces.

2. Fold the rectangles in half, right sides together, where indicated on the pattern pieces.

3. Sew the bow piece on all 3 sides, leaving a small opening for turning. Sew the band (the smaller rectangle) on the long edge.

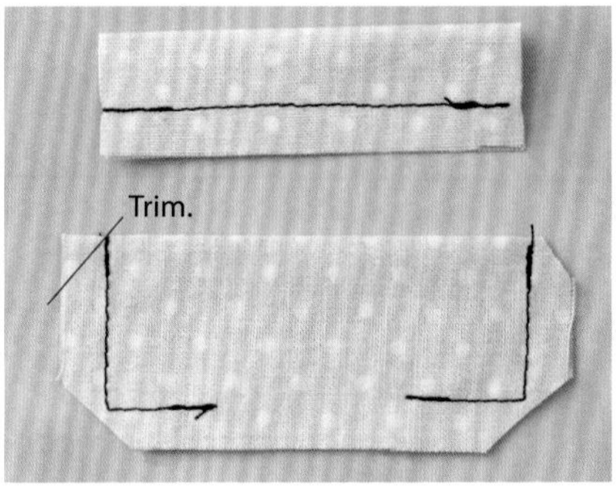

4. Cut the corners of the bow piece diagonally, turn both pieces right side out, and press.

5. Sew the opening of the bow piece closed.

6. Pinch the bow piece in the center and wrap the tie piece around it. Sew across the width of the tie piece and trim the extra fabric.

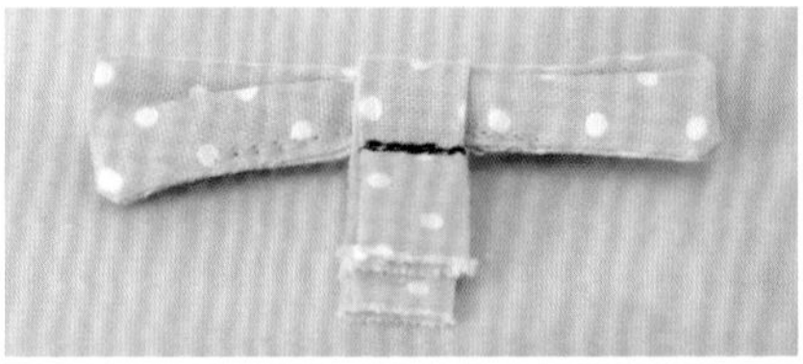

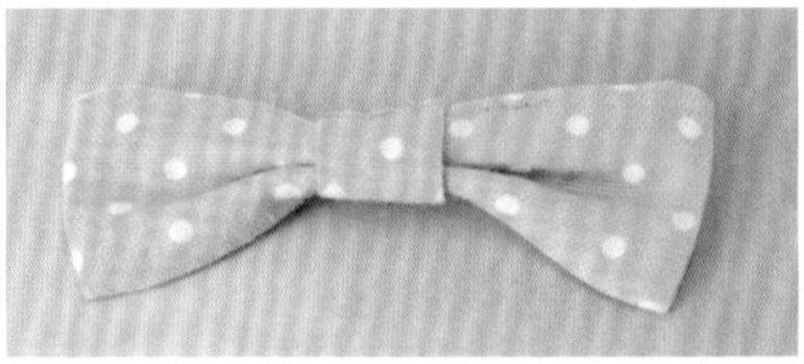

Add an Appliqué

Creating one-of-a-kind designs is quick and easy with raw-edge appliqués. Any line drawing can work, and placement can even be random for a Euro-inspired design. Many fusible web products are permanent and don't require stitching the appliqué in place once it's been fused to the garment.

Materials

Fusible web: 1 small piece a little bigger than the appliqué design

Fabric: 1 scrap a little bigger than the fusible web

Pencil or ultrafine marker

Iron and ironing board

Lightbox or bright window

MAKING AND ATTACHING THE APPLIQUÉ

1. Use a lightbox or sunny window to trace the appliqué design onto the paper side of the fusible web.

tip *If you have an acrylic extension table for quilting (such as a Sew Steady table), you can place a light under it and transform it into an instant lightbox.*

2. Using an iron, fuse the fusible web to the wrong side of the appliqué fabric. Allow it to cool.

3. Carefully cut on the traced line.

4. Peel off the paper backing and position the appliqué onto the right side of the garment fabric.

5. Once the appliqué is positioned, press it with an iron to fuse it to the fabric.

6. *Optional:* Sew around the edges of the appliqué with a satin, blanket, straight, or zigzag stitch.

tip *Use the printed design of the fabric, such as a flower or animal, to create a cute appliqué.*

CHAPTER TWO

Absolutely A-Line Dresses

VIEW C: Pretty Posies. VIEW E: Woodland Wonder. VIEW D: Summer Whimsy.
VIEW B: Posh and Playful. VIEW A: Petite Mademoiselle.

Materials

All views

Dress: ⅓ yard

Lining: 1 fat eighth or ⅛ yard

Closure: 5 buttons (½″ in diameter), 5 snaps, *or* ⅓ yard of hook-and-loop tape

Light- to medium-weight fusible interfacing: 2 pieces 1″ × 8″

Views A and B

Collar/bow/pockets: 1 fat eighth or ¼ yard

View B only: Jeans needle size 14 or 16

View C

Ruffles: ⅛ yard of fabric

Grosgrain ribbon (½″ wide): Substitute 1⅜ yards of ribbon for the ruffles (*optional*).

Views D and E

Underskirt: ¼ yard

Lace and ribbon: 1–3 pieces, ⅔ yard *each*

View D only: 2 buttons (¼″ in diameter)

Cutting

Use the patterns to cut out the fabric pieces (see the pattern pullout for tracing or Patterns, page 7, for downloading and printing instructions). Follow the cutting instructions on the patterns and use a fabric-marking tool to transfer any pattern markings onto the fabric pieces. Use the measurements given below to cut out the remaining pieces needed.

View A

- Front 1, Back 2, Lining Front 3, Lining Back 4, Half-Cap Sleeve 5, Collar A 7, and Bow 10

View B

- Front 1, Back 2, Lining Front 3, Lining Back 4, Cap Sleeve 6, Collar B 8, and Pocket 9

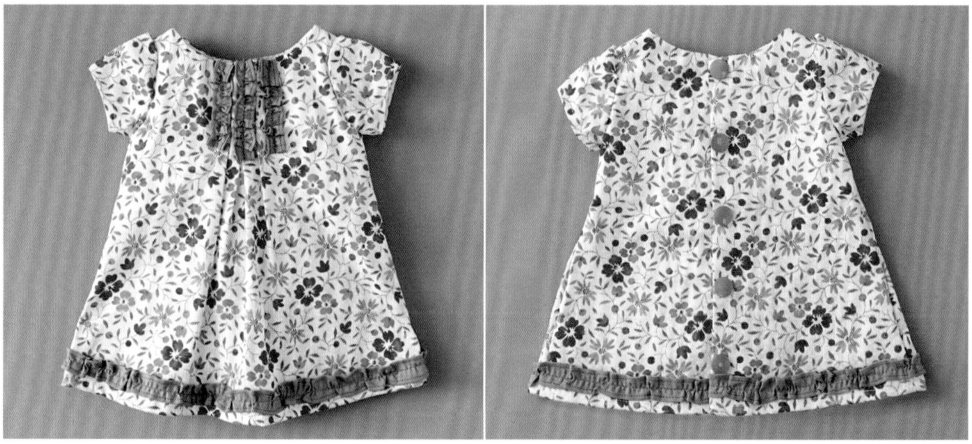

View C

- Front 1, Back 2, Lining Front 3, Lining Back 4, and Cap Sleeve 6
- Ruffles: 1˝ × 34˝ and 1˝ × 15˝ (*Note:* This allows ¼˝ for hem allowances on the long edges of the ruffle pieces.)

View D

- Front 1, Back 2, Lining Front 3, and Lining Back 4
- Underskirt: 6˝ × 28˝

View E

- Front 1, Back 2, Lining Front 3, and Lining Back 4
- Underskirt: 7˝ × 24˝
- Ruffle: 1½˝ × 40˝

Sewing Instructions

All seams are ¼˝ unless otherwise instructed. Finish and press the seam allowances after sewing each seam.

Released Tucks

ALL VIEWS

1. On the dress front, fold and press each tuck, with the 2 center tucks meeting at the center (see Sew a Pleated Skirt, page 14).

tip

Use a piece of painter's tape to hold the tucks in place. It can also be used as a guide to make sure the tucks are stitched to the same length.

2. Sew the tucks, stitching very close to the folded edge and stopping 2˝ down from the top edge. Backstitch at the end of each tuck.

tip

To secure the tucks, leave the thread ends long at the end of each tuck. Pull on the thread from the wrong side of the fabric to pull the top thread to the wrong side. Tie each pair of threads into a knot before trimming them.

Shoulder Seams

ALL VIEWS

1. Sew the dress shoulder seams with right sides together. Press the seam allowances open.

2. Finish the center back edges.

Collar

VIEWS A AND B

1. Sew the collar (see Sew a Collar or Yoke, page 17).

2. Pin and baste the collar to the dress front, both right sides up, and place the triangle notch at the center front of the dress. *Note:* The collar's ends will not be the same distance from each center back edge. This allows for one side to overlap when finished.

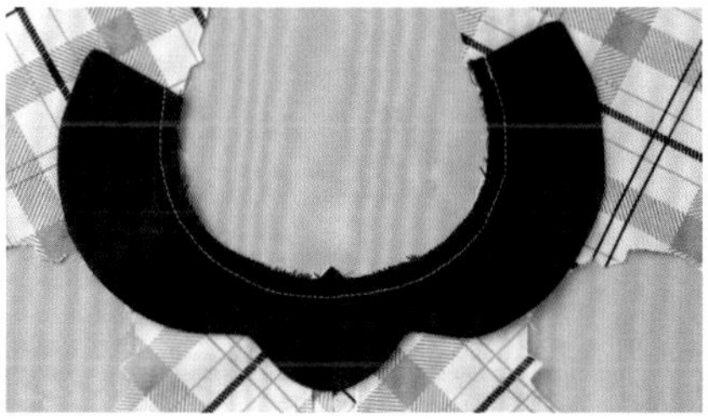

Lining

ALL VIEWS

1. Sew the shoulder seams of the lining pieces with right sides together. Press the seam allowances open.

2. For Views A, B, and C only: Finish the lower edge of the lining.

3. Fold the center back edges of the dress to the right side along the self-facing fold line, as marked by the triangle notches.

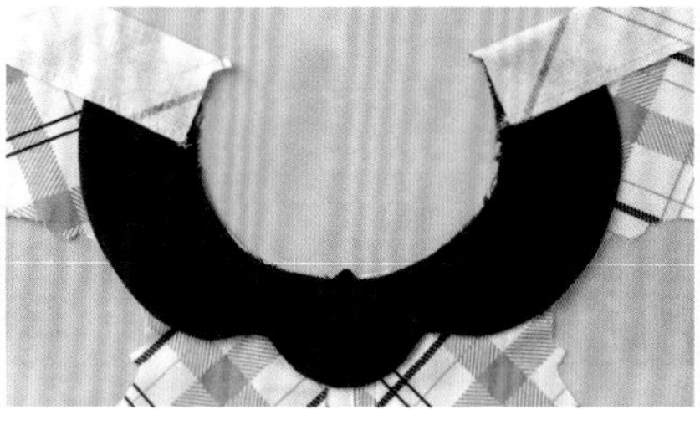

4. Pin and sew the lining to the dress at the neckline, right sides together and on top of the folded self-facing fabric.

5. Clip triangle notches within the seam allowances.

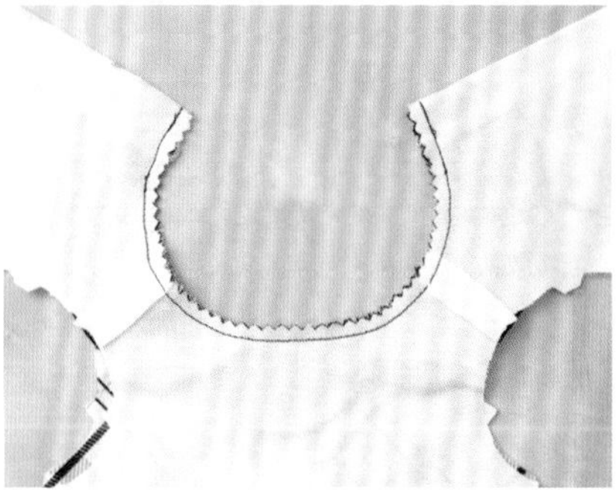

VIEWS B AND C

1. Fold the lining and outer fabric to the inside along the marked self-facing fold line. Press.

2. Baste together at the arm openings and sides, keeping the raw edges even.

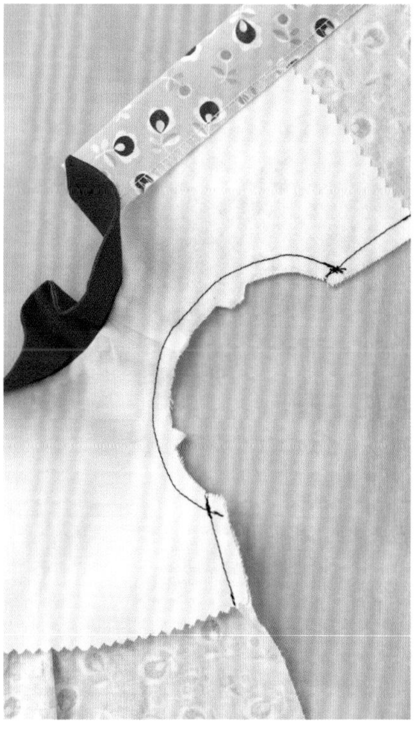

Sleeves

VIEW A

1. Hem the sleeve ends. Sew gathering stitches on the sleeves where indicated on the pattern (see Hemming, page 11), and gather to about 3˝.

2. Fold the collar and lining out of the way. With right sides together, pin and sew the sleeves to the dress where indicated on the pattern.

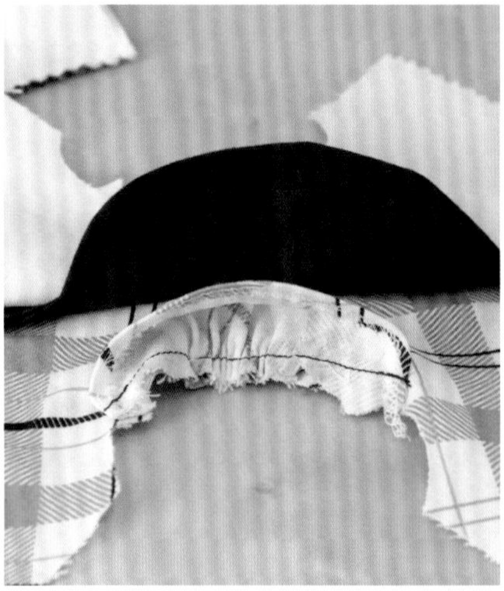

VIEWS A, D, AND E

Pin and sew the dress and lining at the arm opening edges, right sides together. Turn the dress right side out and press. (See Sew a Bodice with Flutter or Half-Cap Sleeves, page 11, or Sew a Lined Bodice Without Sleeves, page 10.)

VIEWS B AND C

1. Hem the sleeve ends (see Hemming, page 11).

2. For View B: Make an inverted box pleat on each sleeve where indicated on the pattern (see Sew a Pleated Skirt, page 14).

For View C: Sew gathering stitches along the sleeve caps and gather to fit the dress.

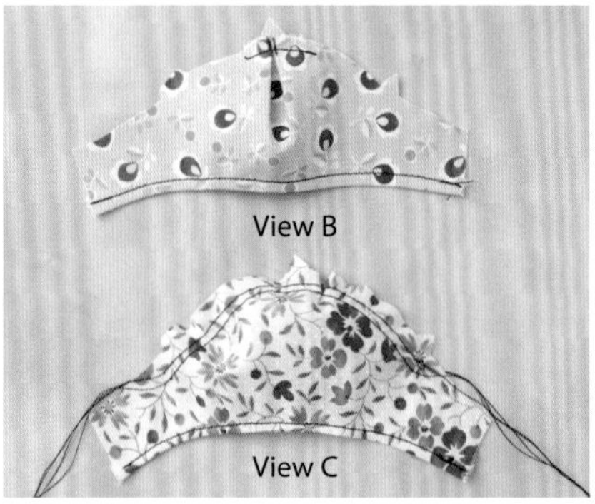

tip *When gathering small pieces such as doll sleeves, you can backstitch at one end and use only the thread at the other end to gather the fabric.*

3. Pin and sew the sleeves to the dress, right sides together.

Side Seams

VIEWS A, D, AND E

Pin and sew the lining and dress together at the sides, right sides together (see Sew a Lined Bodice Without Sleeves, page 10).

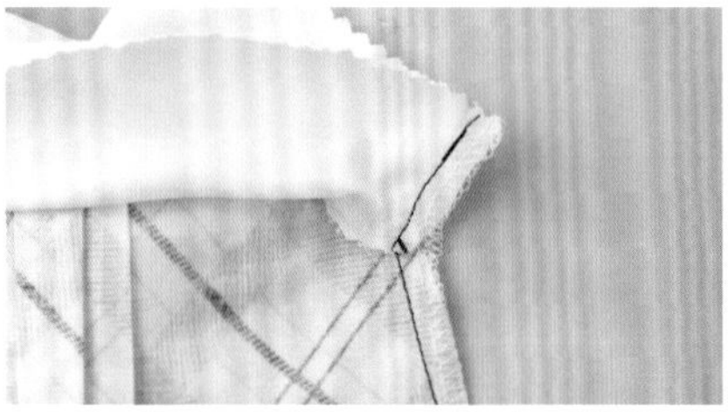

VIEWS B AND C

Pin and sew the side and sleeve seams in one continuous step, with the fabric right sides together and the sleeve hems even.

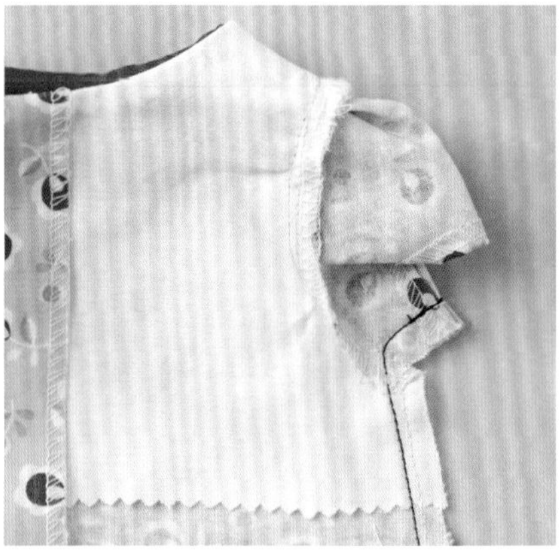

Hem

VIEWS A, B, C, AND D

Hem the lower edge of the dress (see Hemming, page 11).

VIEW E

Hem the dress with trim (see Hemming with Trim, page 12).

VIEWS D AND E

1. Hem the underskirt piece with lace (View D) or a ruffle (View E). See Hemming with Trim (page 12) or Make a Ruffle (page 18).

2. Finish the center back edges of the underskirt.

3. Sew gathering stitches along the upper edge of the underskirt piece and gather it to fit the lining.

4. Pin and sew the underskirt to the lining, with the wrong side of the underskirt facing the right side of the lining. Once sewn, the right sides of the dress and the lining will face up.

5. Finish the seam allowances and press toward the lining.

Center Back Closure

ALL VIEWS

Note: Instead of folding one edge, you will overlap the center back opening.

1. Fuse the interfacing to the wrong side of the self-facing edges.

2. Sew the buttons and buttonholes at the center back where indicated on the pattern piece.

Finishing

VIEW A

Make the bow and sew it to the collar (see Fabric Bow, page 20).

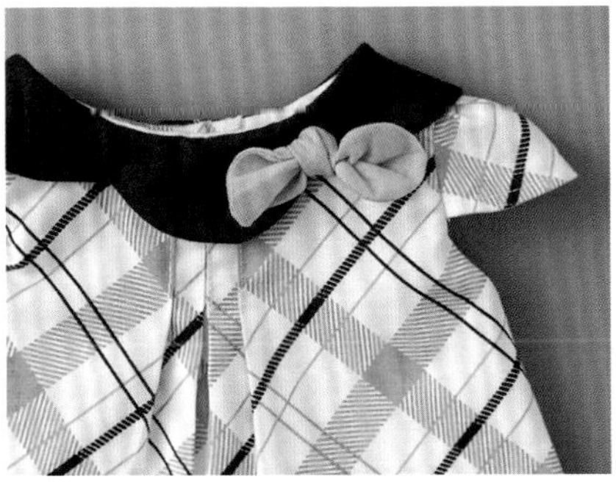

VIEW B

Pocket

1. Sew a basting stitch ¼″ from the raw edge of the round edge. Sew gathering stitches on the straight edge.

2. Fold the rounded edge ¼″ toward the wrong side and press. *Note:* The stitching line enables you to create a nicely rounded edge by keeping the crease of the fold along the basting stitches.

3. Gather the top edge to 2¼″ and bind it with a binding strip (see Finish with Bias Binding, page 11).

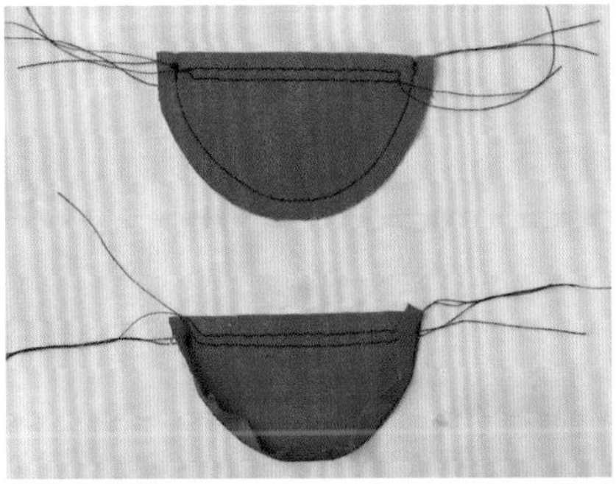

4. Fold the bound upper edge ¼″ toward the wrong side, and re-press, making sure the entire rounded edge is still neatly pressed under.

5. Pin and sew the pocket to the dress where indicated on the pattern piece. Sew slowly over the thick binding layers with a jeans needle size 14 or 16.

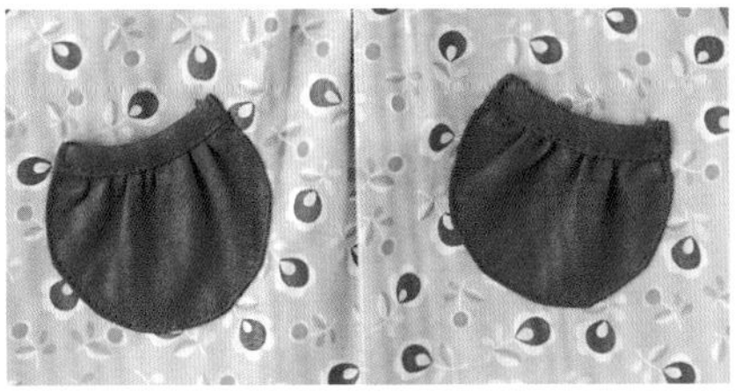

6. Repeat Steps 1–5 to make and attach the second pocket.

VIEW C

1. From the 15″ strip, cut 3 pieces: 2 outer ruffle pieces 4″ long and 1 center ruffle piece 4½″ long.

2. See Make a Ruffle (page 18) to finish the edges and gather the 3 short ruffle pieces to measure 1¾″ for the outer ruffles and 2″ for the center ruffle.

3. Tucking the short ends under, pin and sew the ruffles to the dress with all right sides up.

4. Gather the 34″ ruffle strip to fit the lower edge of the dress.

5. Pin and sew the ruffle to the lower edge of the dress.

VIEW D

Sew buttons to the center of the dress tucks.

VIEW E

Sew additional lace or trims to the hem of the dress.

Spring Meadow

Add the Flutter Sleeve 44 pattern to View E. To make the sleeves, see the Summer Frolic dress (page 57). Follow the View A construction order for sewing the flutter sleeves to the dress and the View E construction order for the rest of the construction.

CHAPTER THREE

Classic Sleeveless Dresses

VIEW A: Art Class. VIEW B: Pink Lemonade. VIEW C: City Girl.
VIEW D: Love Notes. VIEW E: I ❤ Westies. VIEW F: Violet Fields.

Materials

All views

Lining: 1 fat eighth or ⅛ yard

Hook-and-loop tape: ⅛ yard

View A

Bodice: 1 fat eighth or ¼ yard

Left-hand skirt piece and collar: 1 fat eighth or ¼ yard

Right-hand skirt piece: 1 fat eighth or ¼ yard

View B

Bodice: 1 fat eighth or ¼ yard

Patchwork skirt, ruffle, and flower: Small scraps to ⅛ yard *or* 1 fat eighth of 3–6 different fabrics (Use 2½″ precut strips for some!)

Small pom-pom trim: 1 yard

Button (½″ diameter): 1

View C

Bodice and skirt: ⅓ yard

Ruffles* and contrast hem: ⅛ yard of bias-print plaid

View D

Bodice and skirt: ⅓ yard

Skirt insert: ⅛ yard or 1 precut 2½″ strip

Ribbon (⅝″ wide): ½ yard

Appliqués: Various scraps

Paper-backed fusible web

Disappearing fabric marker

Embroidery needle and floss

Anti-fray sealant

French curve ruler (*optional*)

View E

Bodice and skirt: ¼ yard

Contrast hem: ⅛ yard

Appliqués: Various scraps

Paper-backed fusible web

View F

Bodice and skirt: ¼ yard

Ruffle and sash: ⅛ yard

**Substitute ⅝ yard of lace for a faster variation.*

Cutting

Use the patterns to cut out the fabric pieces (see the pattern pullout for tracing or Patterns, page 7, for downloading and printing instructions). Follow the cutting instructions on the patterns and use a fabric-marking tool to transfer any pattern markings onto the fabric pieces. Use the measurements given below to cut out the remaining pieces needed.

View A

- Bodice Front 13, Bodice Back 14, and Collar 15
- Left-hand skirt: 6½″ × 19½″
- Right-hand skirt: 6½″ × 11½″

View B

- Bodice Front 13 and Bodice Back 14
- Patchwork skirt:

  1 piece 4½˝ × 15½˝

  2 pieces 2½˝ × 15½˝ (from 2 different fabrics)

  5 pieces 2½˝ × 6½˝ (from at least 3 different fabrics)
- Flower: 1½˝ × 6½˝
- Ruffle trim: 1½˝ × 42˝

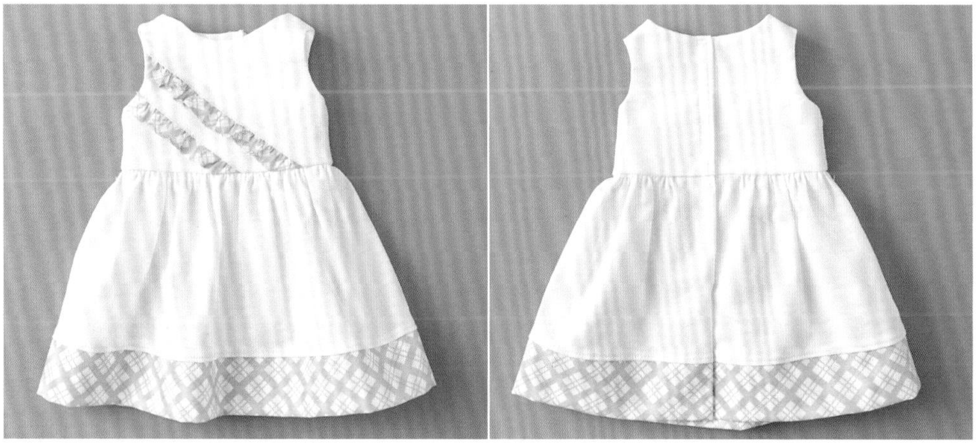

View C

- Bodice Front 13, Bodice Back 14, Bodice Upper Front (A) 16, Bodice Middle Front (B) 17, and Bodice Lower Front (C) 18
- Skirt: 5½˝ × 26˝
- Contrast hem: 3½˝ × 26˝
- Ruffles: 1˝ × 11½˝ and 1˝ × 7¼˝ (¼˝ hem allowance)

View D

- Bodice Front 13, Bodice Back 14, and Love Notes appliqué motifs
- Upper skirt: 4˝ × 26˝
- Middle skirt insert: 2¼˝ × 26˝
- Lower skirt: 1¾˝ × 26˝

View E

- Bodice Front 13, Bodice Back 14, and I ❤ Westies appliqué motifs
- Skirt: 5½″ × 26″
- Contrast hem: 3½″ × 26″

View F

- Bodice Front 13 and Bodice Back 14
- Skirt: 5½″ × 26″
- Ruffle: 1¾″ × 42″
- Sash: 2¼″ × 34″

Sewing Instructions

All seams are ¼″ unless otherwise instructed. Finish and press the seam allowances after sewing each seam.

Bodice Details

VIEW A

Make the collars (see Sew a Collar or Yoke, page 17).

VIEW C

Note: *Sew the pieced bodice front using a scant ¼″ seam allowance (a little less than ¼″) to allow for the bulk of the ruffles. Make sure the ruffles are not gathered within the side seam allowances.*

1. Make 2 ruffle pieces (see Make a Ruffle, page 18).

2. Gather the ruffle pieces, one to fit on the lower edge of the Bodice Upper Front (A) piece and one to fit the lower edge of the Bodice Middle Front (B) piece.

3. Pin and sew the ruffle pieces to the lower edges of the Bodice Upper Front (A) piece and the Bodice Middle Front (B) piece, right sides together.

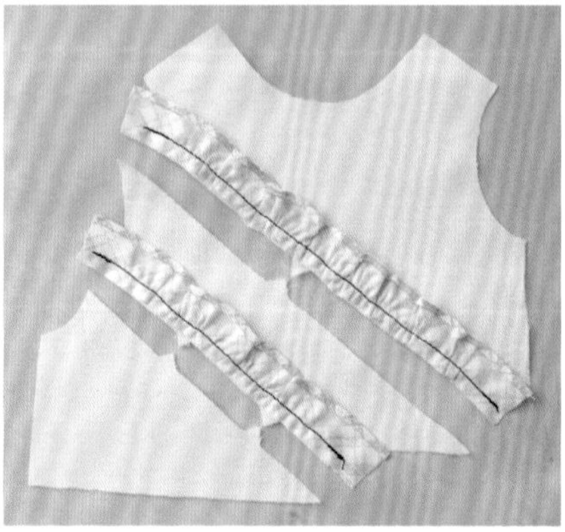

Make sure the ruffle pieces extend a little past the bodice pieces, as shown.

4. Pin and sew the Bodice Middle Front (B) piece to the Bodice Upper Front (A) piece, right sides together and with the ruffle sandwiched in the middle.

5. Pin and sew the bodice A/B unit to the Bodice Lower Front (C) piece, right sides together and with the ruffle sandwiched in the middle.

6. Press the seam allowances up toward the neckline and the ruffles down toward the waist.

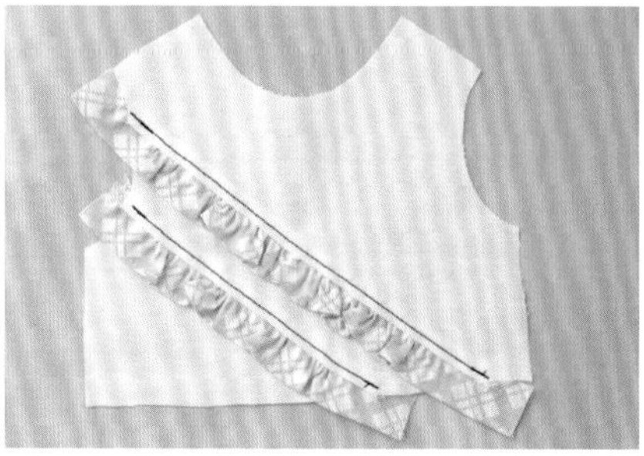

7. Edgestitch along the bodice just above the ruffles. Trim the excess ruffles from the bodice front to match the front lining piece.

Bodice

ALL VIEWS

Sew the lined bodice (see Sew a Lined Bodice Without Sleeves, page 10).

Skirt

VIEW A

Pin and sew the left- and right-hand skirt pieces with right sides together.

VIEW B

1. Sew the 2 different 2½″ × 15½″ pieces right sides together along the long edges. Press the seam allowances toward the piece you want at the top of the skirt.

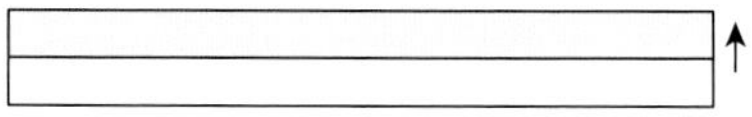

2. Sew the unit from Step 1 to the 4½″ × 15½″ piece, right sides together, as shown. Press the seam allowances toward the larger piece.

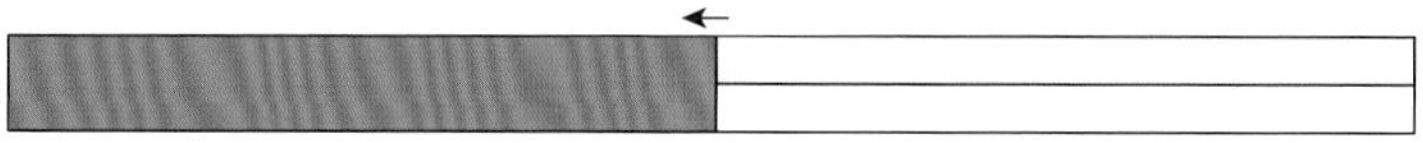

3. Sew all the 2½″ × 6½″ pieces right sides together along the short ends to make 1 long strip. Press the finished seam allowances all in the same direction.

4. Sew the strip from Step 3 to the lower edge of the unit from Step 2, right sides together. Press the finished seam allowances up.

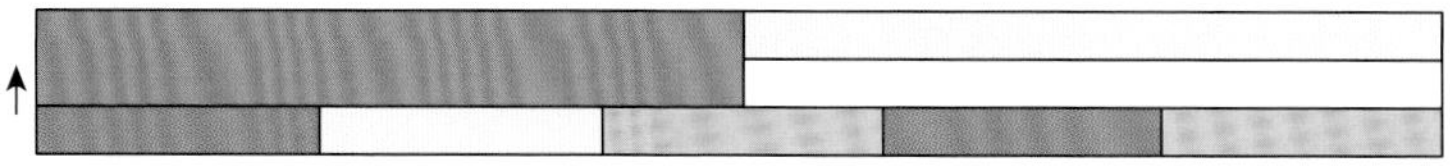

VIEW D

1. Trace the Love Notes embroidery design (pattern pullout page P1) with a disappearing fabric marker on the contrast middle-skirt piece.

tip *You can also use a French curve to draw your own curved-line design.*

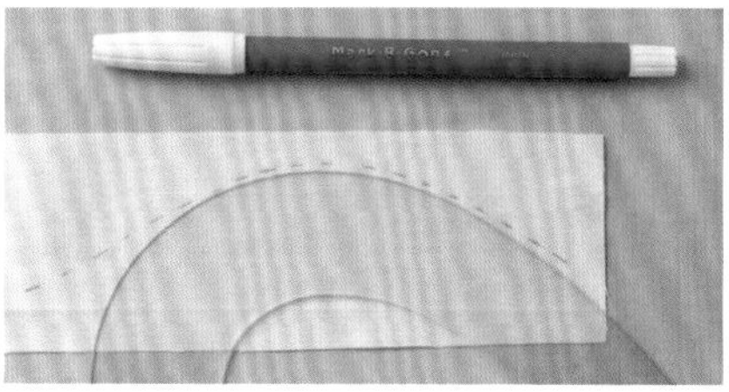

2. Fuse and sew the appliqués to the middle skirt piece (see Add an Appliqué, page 20).

3. Use embroidery floss and a needle to sew a running stitch design on the envelopes and on the drawn stitching line.

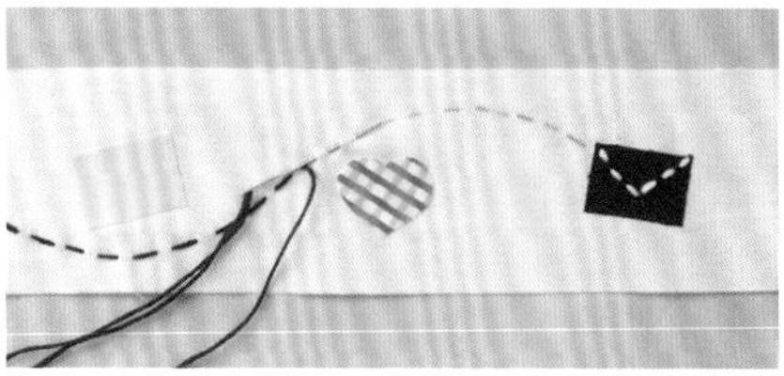

Keep the design centered and clear of the ¼″ seam allowance.

tip *To prevent the thread from knotting and tangling while hand sewing, run a hot iron over it. It will take out the moisture so the thread tangles less. This is especially important for those who live in humid climates.*

4. Sew the 3 skirt pieces right sides together and press the finished seam allowances toward the dark fabric.

VIEW E

Add the appliqué design to the lower edge of the skirt piece (see Add an Appliqué, page 20), fusing the body piece first and then the face, eyes, and nose pieces on top. *Note:* Fuse and sew the Westie's paws after the contrast hem has been sewn to the skirt piece.

VIEWS C AND E

Sew the contrast hem (see Sewing a Contrast Hem, page 12).

VIEW F

Sew the ruffle hem (see Make a Ruffle, page 18).

ALL VIEWS

Sew the skirt to the bodice (see Gathered Skirts, page 14).

For View A: Place the skirt seam where indicated on the pattern piece.

For View B: Center the upper skirt seam on the bodice front.

Center Back Closure

ALL VIEWS

Sew the center back seam and closure (see Center Back Seam and Closures, page 16).

Hemming

VIEWS A AND D

Sew a narrow hem (see Hemming, page 11).

VIEW B

Hem the skirt with small pom-pom trim (see Hemming with Trim, page 12).

tip

Use a zipper foot and adjust the needle position to make it easier to sew the pom-pom trim.

Finishing

VIEW B

1. Make a ruffle detail and sew it to the skirt piece (see Make a Ruffle, page 18).

2. Sew together the short ends of the flower piece with right sides together, forming a loop. Press the seam allowances open.

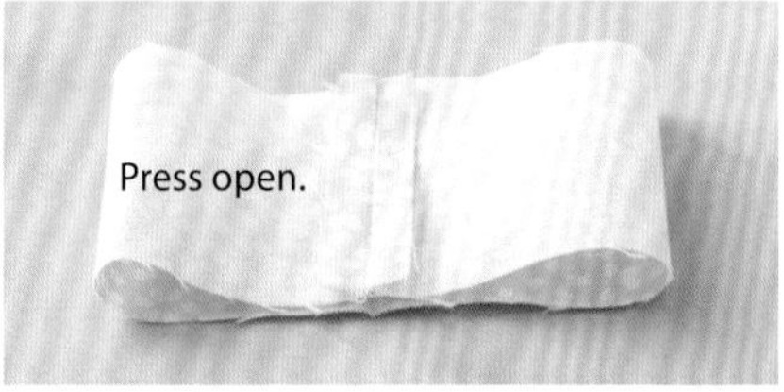

3. Fold the fabric loop in half, wrong sides together. Keep its loop shape.

4. Using a thread and needle, hand sew a running stitch along the raw edges without knotting the thread. Keep the ends long.

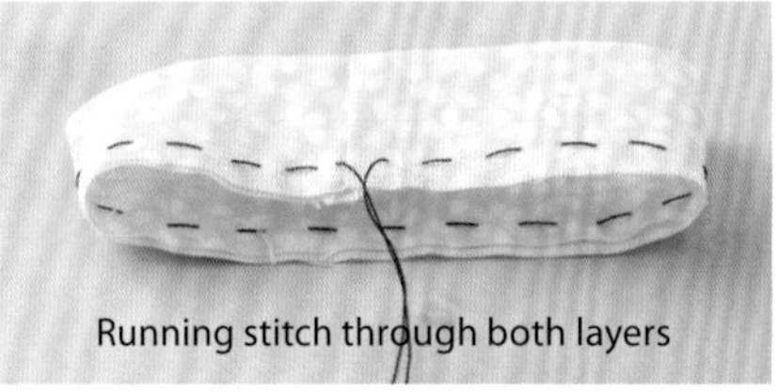

5. Pull the thread ends together until the center of the loop is all gathered up into a disk. Knot and trim the thread ends.

6. Sew the flower onto the waist with a button.

VIEW D

1. Cut the ends of the velvet ribbon at a diagonal and use anti-fray sealant to keep the ribbon from fraying.

2. Using a needle and embroidery floss, sew the velvet ribbon to the waistband using a herringbone stitch, as shown below. Make sure to leave about 12˝ tails at the center back to tie into a bow.

The Herringbone Stitch

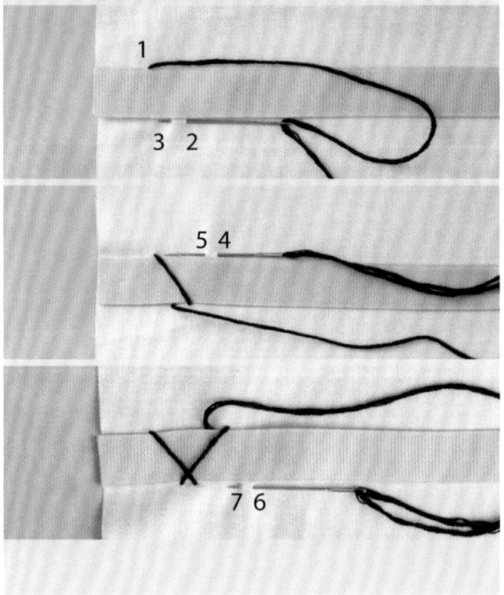

Freshly Picked

Cat's Meow

Use the additional appliqué patterns to create two other unique designs. For the bodice on Freshly Picked, add a little appliqué on the bodice front. Sew the dresses in the same manner as View E.

CHAPTER FOUR

Country Cottage Dresses

VIEW A: Summer Picnic. VIEW B: Bluebell. VIEW C: Rosebud.
VIEW D: May Day. VIEW E: Hootenanny. VIEW F: Hopscotch.

Materials

All views

Bodice and sleeves: 1 fat quarter or ¼ yard

Waistband: Scrap of complementary fabric

Knit elastic (¼″ wide): ½ yard

Hook-and-loop tape: ¼ yard

View A

Skirt: 1 fat quarter or ¼ yard

Ruffle: ⅛ yard of complementary fabric

View B

Skirt: 1 fat quarter or ¼ yard

Center gores: Scrap of complementary fabric, approximately 9″ × 10″

Velvet ribbon (⅛″ wide): ½ yard

View C

Skirt: 1 fat quarter or ¼ yard

Center gores: Scrap of solid fabric, approximately 9″ × 10″

Lace: 1½ yards

Assorted ribbons and trims: ⅓-yard pieces

View D

Skirt and ruffle: ½ yard

Velvet ribbon (¼″ wide): 1⅛ yards

Velvet ribbon (⅛″ wide): ½ yard

View E

Skirt: ⅛ yard *each* for 3 tiers (2½″-precut-strip friendly!)

Lace: 1¼ yards

View F

Skirt: 1 fat quarter or ⅓ yard

Lace: ½ yard

Cutting

Use the patterns to cut out the fabric pieces (see the pattern pullout for tracing or Patterns, page 7, for downloading and printing instructions). Follow the cutting instructions on the patterns and use a fabric-marking tool to transfer any pattern markings onto the fabric pieces. Use the measurements given below to cut out the remaining pieces needed.

View A

- Bodice Front 19, Bodice Back 20, Raglan Sleeve 21, and Skirt Gore 22
- Waistband: 1¼″ × 12½″
- Ruffle: 1¾″ × 40″

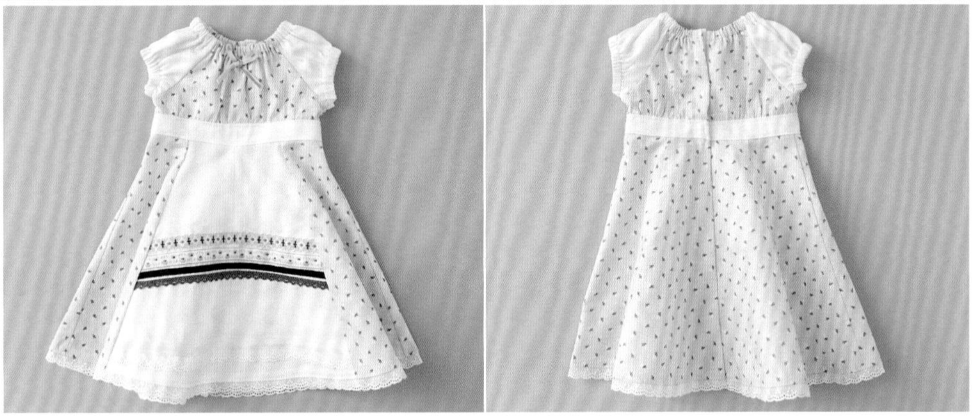

Views B and C

- Bodice Front 19, Bodice Back 20, Raglan Sleeve 21, and Skirt Gore 22
- Waistband: 1¼˝ × 12½˝

View D

- Bodice Front 19, Bodice Back 20, Raglan Sleeve 21, and Skirt Piece 23
- Waistband: 1½˝ × 12½˝
- Ruffle: 1¾˝ × 60˝

**Make this dress without the ruffle hem by using the longer length provided on the skirt pattern.*

View E

- Bodice Front 19, Bodice Back 20, and Raglan Sleeve 21
- Waistband: 1⅞˝ × 12½˝
- Top skirt tier: 2½˝ × 18½˝
- Middle skirt tier: 2½˝ × 27½˝
- Bottom skirt tier: 2½˝ × 42½˝

View F

- Bodice Front 19, Bodice Back 20, Raglan Sleeve 21, and Skirt Piece 23
- Waistband: 1½″ × 12½″

Sewing Instructions

All seams are ¼″ unless otherwise instructed. Finish and press the seam allowances after sewing each seam.

Sleeves

VIEWS A, B, C, AND F

Make casings on the sleeve ends (see Casing Techniques, page 13).

VIEW F

Sew edging trim to the outside edge of the casing, making certain that the casing is still wide enough for the elastic.

VIEWS D AND E

Sew narrow hems on the sleeve ends (see Hemming, page 11).

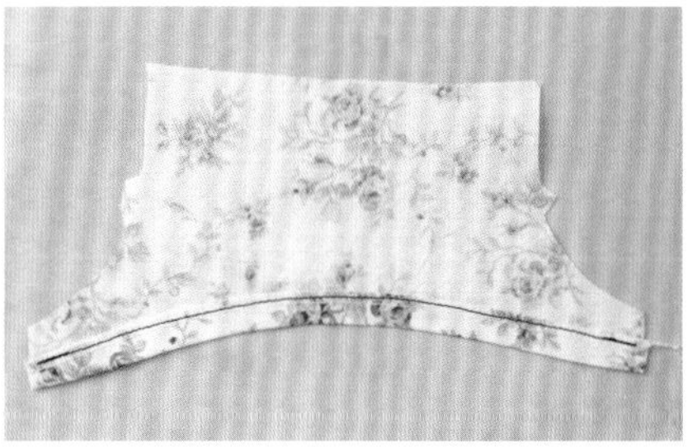

Sewing the Sleeves to the Bodice

ALL VIEWS

1. Sew the sleeves to the bodice front, right sides together. Match the notches.

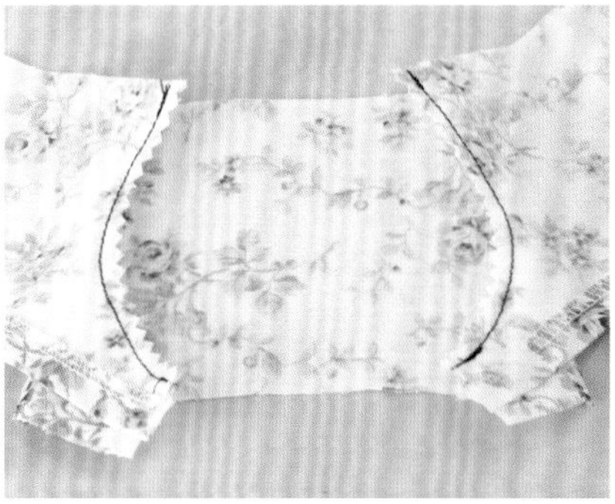

2. Sew the sleeves to the bodice back pieces, right sides together. Match the notches.

Neckline Casing

ALL VIEWS

Make a casing at the neckline edge (see Casing Techniques, page 13). On the casing, stop and start sewing on the dot markings at the bodice back where indicated on the pattern.

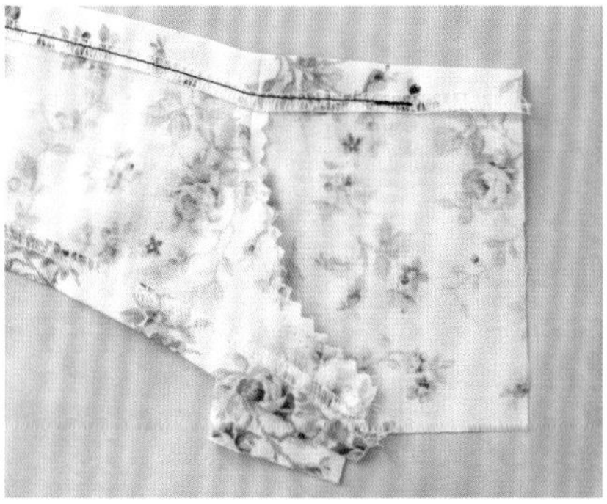

Finishing the Sleeves

VIEWS A, B, C, AND F

Cut 2 pieces of elastic, each 4″ long, and insert them into the sleeve casings (see Inserting Elastic into the Casing, page 13).

VIEW D AND E

1. Cut 2 pieces of elastic, each 3½˝ long.

2. Pin and sew the elastic in place with a zigzag stitch, ⅜˝ from the hemmed edge. Stretch the elastic as you sew (see Elastic Sewn Directly to the Fabric, page 13).

Side Seams and Waistband

ALL VIEWS

1. Pin and sew the side and sleeve seams in a continuous step, with right sides together and the sleeve hems even.

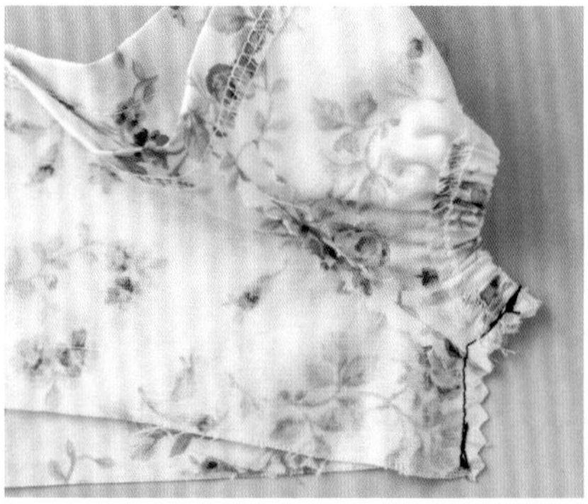

2. Sew gathering stitches along the lower edge of the bodice and gather to fit the waistband. Distribute the gathers evenly; the bodice front will measure about 5½˝. *Note:* Mark and pin together the center points of the waistband and bodice front; then gather to fit.

3. Pin and sew the bodice to the waistband with right sides together, using a ⅜˝ seam allowance.

4. Press the finished seam allowances down toward the waistband.

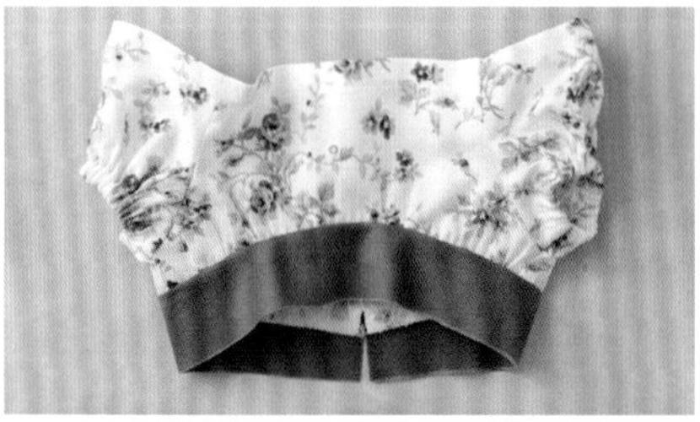

Neckline Elastic

ALL VIEWS

1. Cut a piece of elastic 8˝–8½˝ long, and insert it into the neckline casing, securing the elastic at the dot markings (see Casing Techniques, page 13).

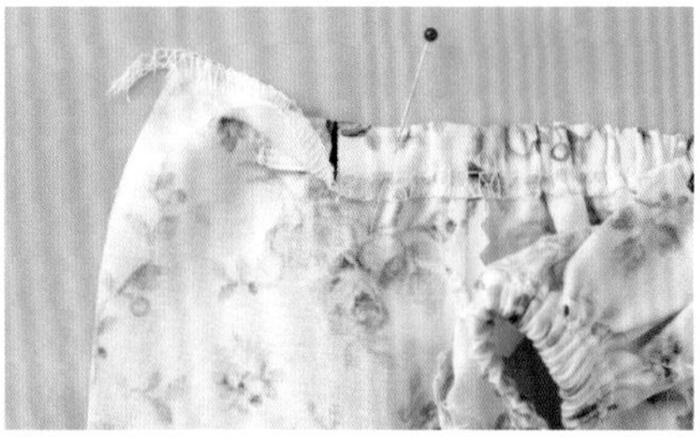

2. Sew the remainder of the casing closed.

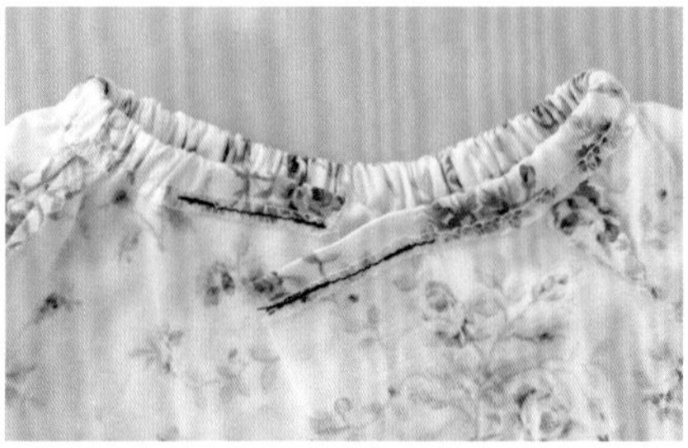

Skirt

VIEW C

1. Pin and sew together the 2 center gores, right sides together.

2. Embellish the right side of the center gores with various trims.

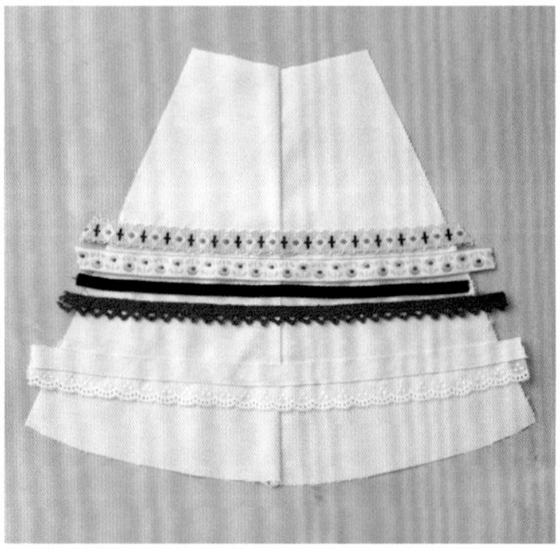

VIEWS A, B, AND C

Sew the skirt gores right sides together, leaving the center back completely open. Make sure that Views B and C have the center gores placed correctly for the skirt design.

tip

Directional sewing is best when sewing garments. A rule of thumb for directional sewing is to always sew widest to narrowest and to sew all the pieces in the same direction.

For example, these gores are wider at the hem than at the waist edge. Directional sewing dictates that you would sew all these gores from hem to waist. Sewing some from waist to hem may stretch or distort the fabric in opposing ways, negatively affecting the drape of the skirt.

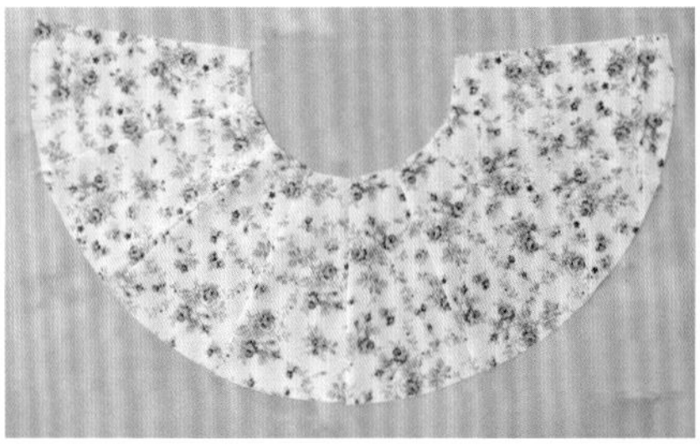

VIEW E

1. Hem the bottom tier with lace (see Hemming with Trim, page 12).

2. Sew gathering stitches on the upper edges of the middle and lower tiers.

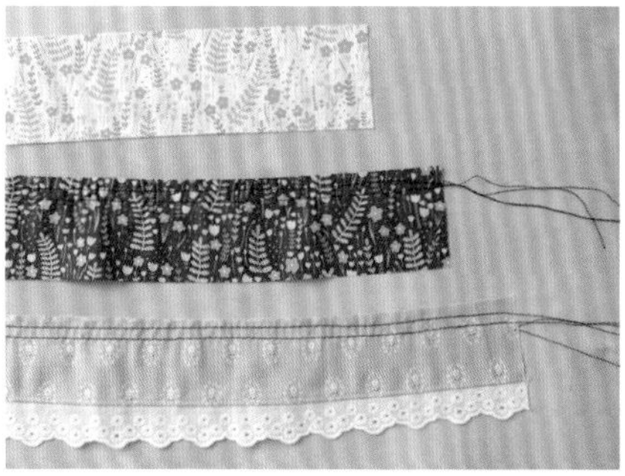

3. Gather to fit. The middle tier should fit the lower edge of the top tier (18½˝), and the bottom tier should fit the lower edge of the middle tier (27½˝).

tip

Try gathering each piece to the needed measurement and evenly distributing the gathers before pinning together the pieces. This will save you a lot of time, especially when adding the final tier to the skirt piece.

4. Pin and sew the upper edge of the middle tier to the lower edge of the top tier.

5. Pin and sew the upper edge of the lower tier to the lower edge of the middle tier.

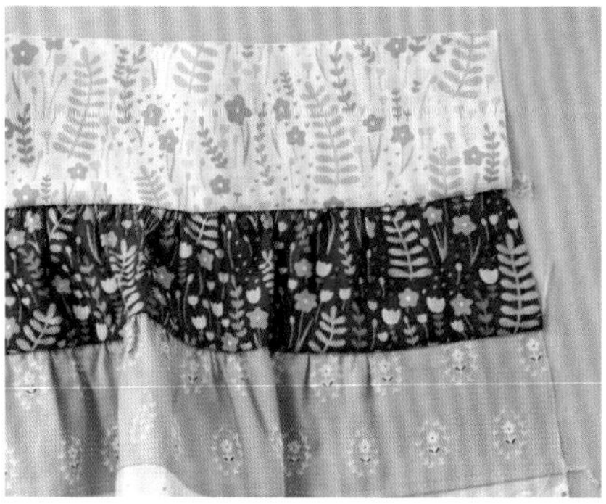

6. Press the finished seam allowances up toward the waistband.

Sewing the Skirt to the Waistband

ALL VIEWS

Pin and sew the skirt piece to the lower edge of the waistband with right sides together, using a ⅜˝ seam allowance.

For View E: Gather the skirt to fit the waistband before sewing the skirt piece to the waistband.

Hemming the Skirt

VIEWS A AND D

Sew the ruffle hem (see Make a Ruffle, page 18).

For View D: Sew the ¼˝-wide ribbon on the skirt, just above the ruffle.

VIEW B

Sew a narrow hem (see Hemming, page 11) after sewing the center back seam.

VIEWS C AND E

Hem the skirt with lace (see Hemming with Trim, page 12).

Center Back Seam and Closure

ALL VIEWS

Sew the center back seam and back closure (see Center Back Seam and Closures, page 16). *Note:* If using hook-and-loop tape, use 3 shorter pieces instead of 1 long piece and place a ¾˝ piece at the waistband, a longer piece at the top, and another on the skirt. This allows the bodice to retain its blousy look.

Finishing

VIEWS B AND D

Sew the ⅛˝-wide ribbon to the waistband.

VIEWS B, C, D, AND E

Sew tiny ribbon bows to the sleeves, waist, and/or neckline.

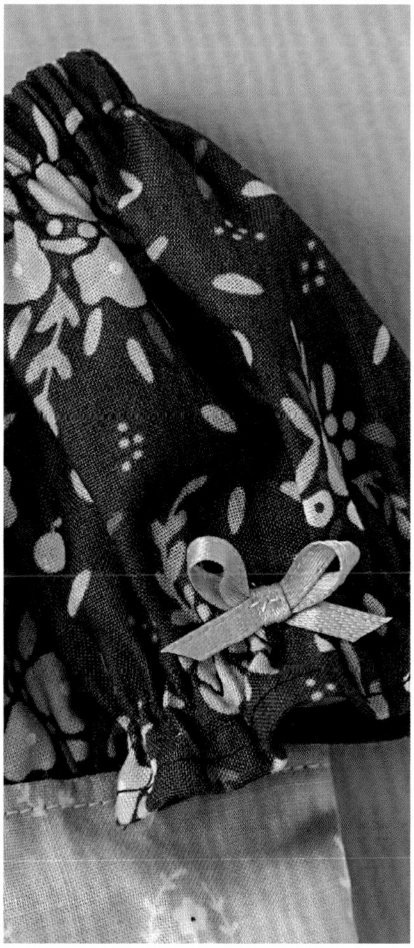

Country Charm

Nothing says "country" more than a gingham check. Use a small-scale gingham for the top and a simple gathered skirt (30˝ × 6˝) to create this cute dress.

Scrap-Happy Hootenanny

Use a mini charm square pack (2½˝ × 2½˝ precut squares) or scraps cut to size to make this adorable variation, in which you sew together the squares to create the tiers in View E. Precut squares make this super quick: Not only are they precut but they also have pinked edges that won't need to be finished.

Tier 1: 9 squares

Tier 2: 13 squares

Tier 3: 21 squares

Sew together the dress in the same manner as View E.

CHAPTER FIVE

Square-Neck Dresses

VIEW A: Sunny Day. VIEW B: Cape Cod.
VIEW C: Nantucket. VIEW D: Twice as Nice.
VIEW E: Pretty Tucks.

Materials

All views

Dress: ½ yard

Lining: 1 fat eighth or ¼ yard

Hook-and-loop tape: ¼ yard

View A

Buttons (½˝ diameter): 2

Cluny edging lace or picot trim (¼˝ wide): 1¼ yards

View B

Ribbon (⅜˝ wide): 1¾ yards

Ribbon (⅝˝ wide): ⅝ yard

View C

Ribbon (¼˝ wide): 3 yards

View D

Beading lace trim: 2½ yards

Ribbon (to lace through trim if not pre-laced): 2½ yards

View E

Bib: Scrap of fabric

Buttons (¼˝ diameter): 3

Cluny edging lace (⅜˝ wide): 1¼ yards

Cutting

Use the patterns to cut out the fabric pieces (see the pattern pullout for tracing or Patterns, page 7, for downloading and printing instructions). Follow the cutting instructions on the patterns and use a fabric-marking tool to transfer any pattern markings onto the fabric pieces. Use the measurements given below to cut out the remaining pieces needed.

View A

- Bodice Front 24, Bodice Back 25, Sleeve 26, and Bodice Detail 27
- Skirt: 5⅝˝ × 31˝

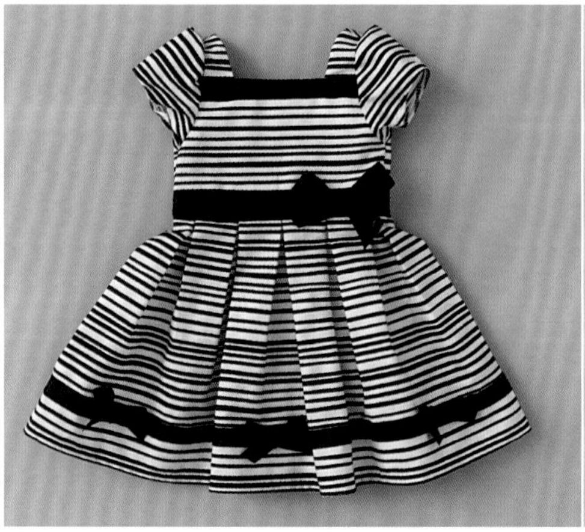

View B

- Bodice Front 24, Bodice Back 25, and Sleeve 26
- Skirt: 7˝ × 31˝

View C

- Bodice Front 24, Bodice Back 25, and Sleeve 26
- Skirt: 7″ × 30″

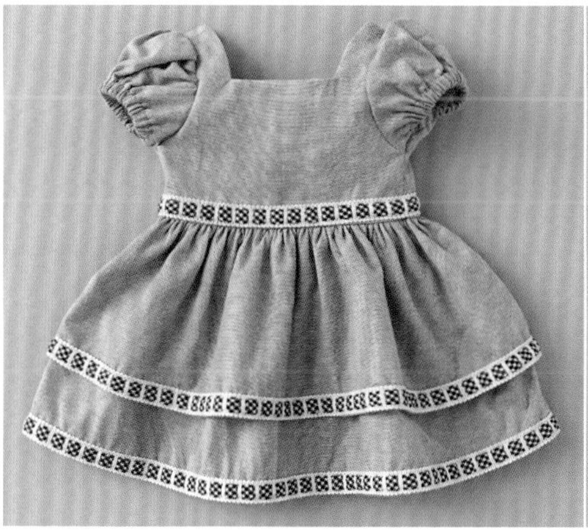

View D

- Bodice Front 24, Bodice Back 25, and Sleeve 28
- Overskirt: 4⅝″ × 28″
- Underskirt: 6⅜″ × 28″

View E

- Bodice Front 24, Bodice Back 25, Sleeve 28, and Bib 29
- Skirt: 9½″ × 30″

Sewing Instructions

All seams are ¼˝ unless otherwise instructed. Finish and press the seam allowances after sewing each seam.

Bib

VIEW E

1. Fold where indicated on the bib pattern, press, and sew each tuck by sewing a scant ¼˝ from the crease in each fold (see Sew a Pleated Skirt, page 14).

2. Press the tucks away from the center.

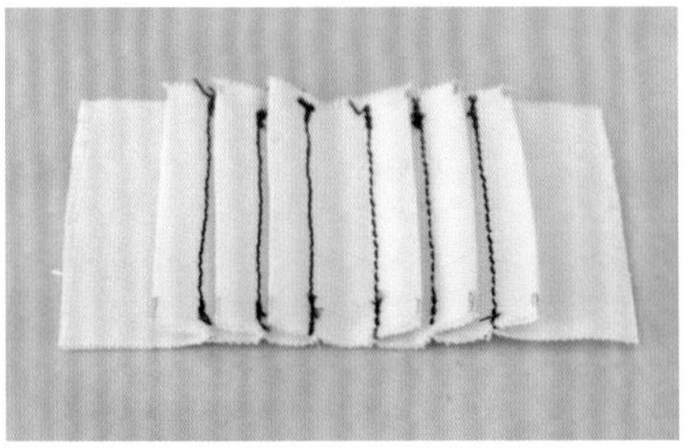

3. Fold and press the lower edge and side edges ¼˝ to the wrong side. The finished width should measure 2⅛˝.

4. Sew the bib to the bodice front, with the wrong side of the bib facing the right side of the bodice.

Bodice

ALL VIEWS

Sew the lined bodice (see Sew a Lined Bodice with Sleeves, page 9).

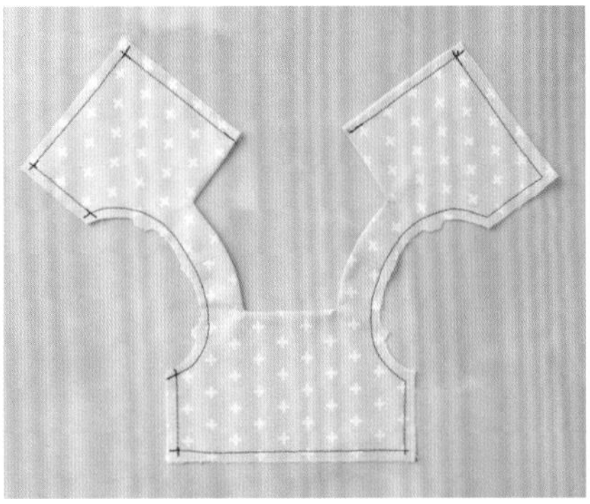

VIEWS B AND C

Topstitch the ribbon to the neckline.

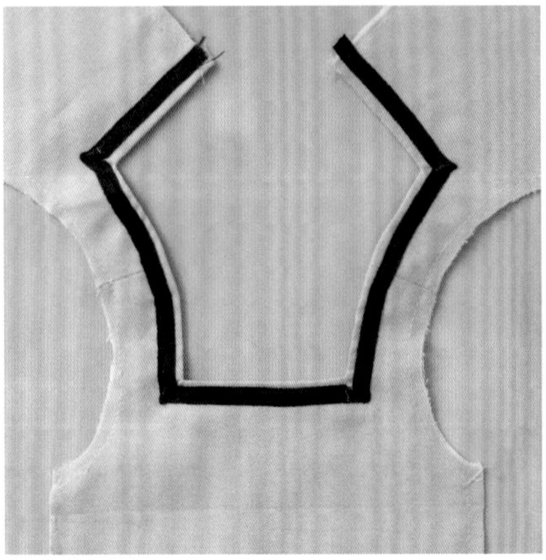

Sleeves

VIEW A

Hem the sleeve ends with edging trim (see Hemming with Trim, page 12).

VIEWS B AND C

Sew narrow hems on the sleeve ends (see Hemming, page 11).

VIEWS D AND E

Sew casings on the sleeve ends (see Casing Techniques, page 13).

VIEW E

Sew edging trim to the wrong side of the sleeve casings. Make sure to sew on the very edge to ensure that the casing is still wide enough for the elastic and safety pin to fit inside.

ALL VIEWS

1. Sew gathering stitches along the sleeve caps where indicated on the pattern, and gather the sleeves to fit the bodice.

2. Pin and sew the sleeves to the bodice, right sides together.

VIEWS D AND E

Cut 2 pieces of elastic, each 4″ long, and insert them into the sleeve casings (see Casing Techniques, page 13).

Side Seams

ALL VIEWS

Pin and sew the sleeve and side seams in one continuous step with right sides together, keeping the sleeve hems even.

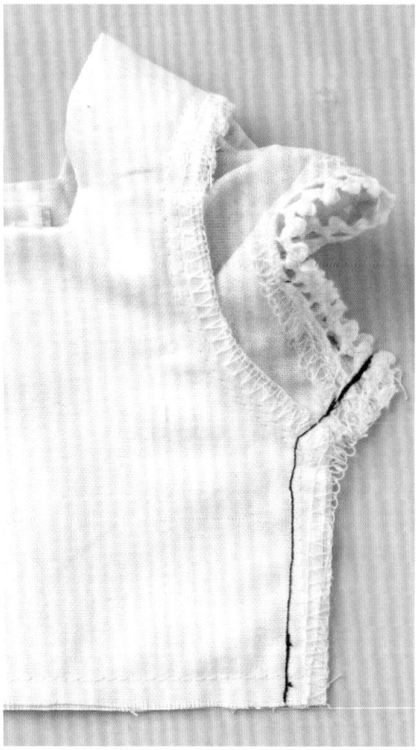

Skirt

VIEW B

Pin and sew the ribbon onto the skirt, 2″ from the lower edge.

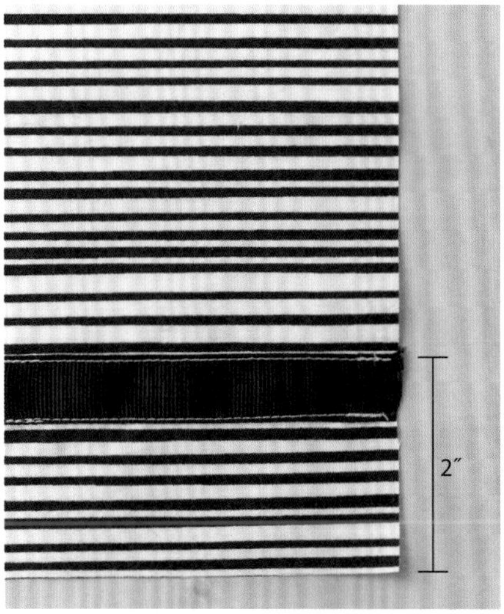

VIEWS A AND B

Fold, press, and baste inverted box pleats on the skirt piece (see Sew a Pleated Skirt, page 14).

VIEW C

Pin and sew ribbons to the skirt piece at 2¼″ and 4¼″ from the lower edge.

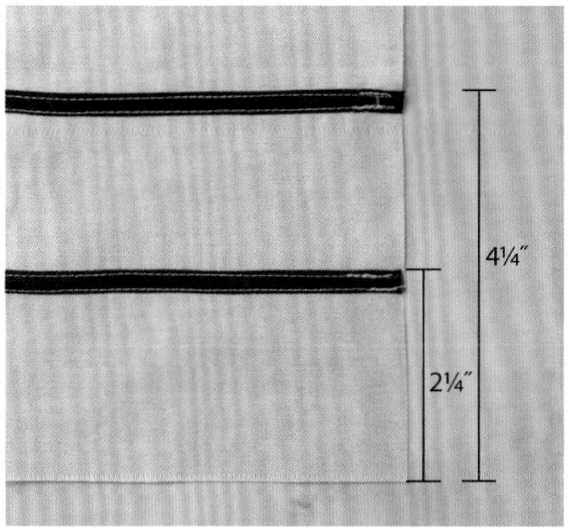

tip *Use fabric glue or Wonder Tape to hold the ribbons in place instead of pins.*

VIEW E

1. Mark the horizontal fold lines for the tucked skirt design: 1¼″, 2⅜″, and 3½″ from the lower edge.

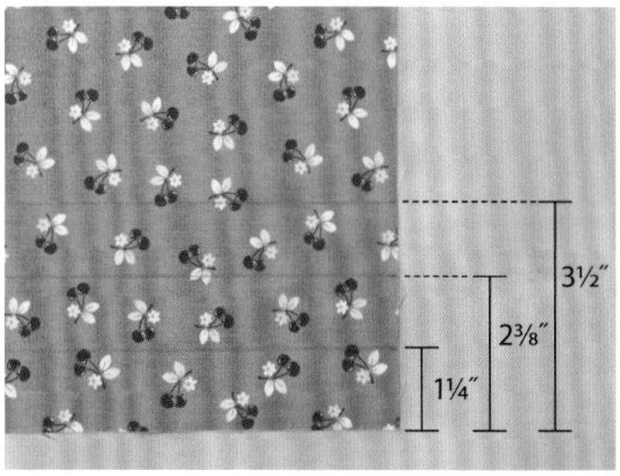

2. Fold, press, and sew each tuck, ⅜″ from the crease of the fold.

3. Press all the tucks down toward the lower edge.

VIEW D

1. Sew narrow hems on the skirt pieces (see Hemming, page 11).

2. If the beading lace trim is not pre-laced, lace ribbon through it. Sew the trim to the right side of the hemmed edges.

ALL VIEWS

Sew the skirt to the bodice.

For Views C, D, and E: See Gathered Skirts (page 14) and Sew a Double-Layered Skirt (page 16).

VIEW D

Sew beading trim to the waist, folding the ends to the wrong side ½˝ from the center back edges.

Center Back Opening

ALL VIEWS

Sew the center back seam and closure (see Center Back Seam and Closures, page 16).

Hem

VIEWS A AND E

Hem the skirt with edging trim (see Hemming with Trim, page 12).

VIEWS B AND C

Sew a narrow hem (see Hemming, page 11).

Finishing

VIEW A

1. Sew together the bodice detail (see Fabric Bow, page 20).

2. Use the buttons to sew the bodice detail onto the bodice.

VIEW B AND C

Sew ribbon bows on the bodice and skirt.

VIEW E

Sew buttons on the bib.

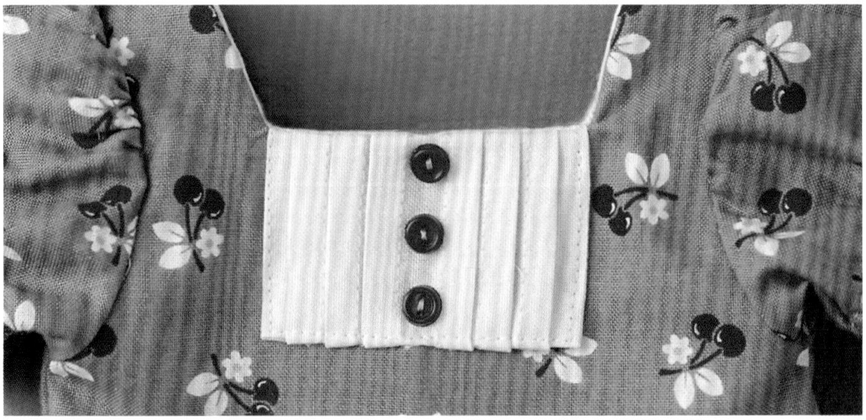

Bright Tulips

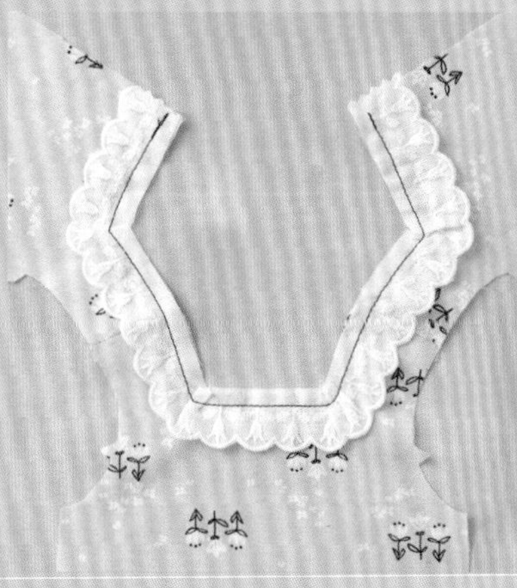

Make this dress by sewing lace to the right side of the bodice before sewing the bodice and lining together.

Using the same skirt measurement as View A, gather the skirt and hem it with a ruffle. Use the Sleeve 28 pattern, binding the sleeves instead of an elastic finish. Tie a ribbon around the waist to finish this bright and cheery design.

Ice Cream Social

Make the square-neck dress sleeveless for a perfect sundress (see Sew a Lined Bodice Without Sleeves, page 10). Use trims in different ways to create this super-fun skirt design!

1. Cut 2 pieces of fabric for the skirt: 1½˝ × 30˝ for the lower part and 5˝ × 30˝ for the upper part.

2. Baste the rickrack to the lower edge of the bodice before sewing the skirt to the bodice.

3. Baste the rickrack to the lower edge of the upper skirt before sewing together the skirt pieces.

4. Hem the skirt with rickrack (see Hemming with Trim, page 12).

CHAPTER SIX

Party Dresses

View B, back; View A, back

VIEW B: Ruffles and Lace. VIEW A: Tea Party.

Materials

All views

Dress: ⅝ yard

Underskirt: ¼ yard

Hook-and-loop tape: ¼ yard

Lace trim (1″–1½″ wide): 1 yard

View A

Lining: 1 fat eighth or ¼ yard of lightweight fabric

Packaged seam binding tape

Ribbon (⅛″ wide): 1 yard

Knit elastic (¼″ wide): ¼ yard

Anti-fray sealant *(optional)*

View B

Ruffle and bias trim: 1 fat quarter or ⅓ yard of complementary fabric

Buttons (⅜″ diameter): 5

Cutting

Use the patterns to cut out the fabric pieces (see the pattern pullout for tracing or Patterns, page 7, for downloading and printing instructions). Follow the cutting instructions on the patterns and use a fabric-marking tool to transfer any pattern markings onto the fabric pieces. Use the measurements given below to cut out the remaining pieces needed.

View A

- Bodice Front 30, Bodice Back 31, and Sleeve 32
- Underskirt: 7¼″ × 30″
- Overskirt: 7½″ × 30″
- Seam binding tape: 2 pieces 5″ long

View B

- Bodice Front 33, Bodice Back 34, and Sleeve 32
- Underskirt: 7¼″ × 30″
- Overskirt: 7¼″ × 30″
- Neckline ruffle: 1½″ × 22″
- Bias trim (strips cut on the bias):

  Neckline: 1 piece 1¼″ × 14″

  Sleeves: 2 pieces 1¼″ × 5¼″

Sewing Instructions

All seams are ¼˝ unless otherwise instructed. Finish and press the seam allowances after sewing each seam.

Bodice

VIEW A

Sew the lined bodice (see Sew a Lined Bodice with Sleeves, page 9).

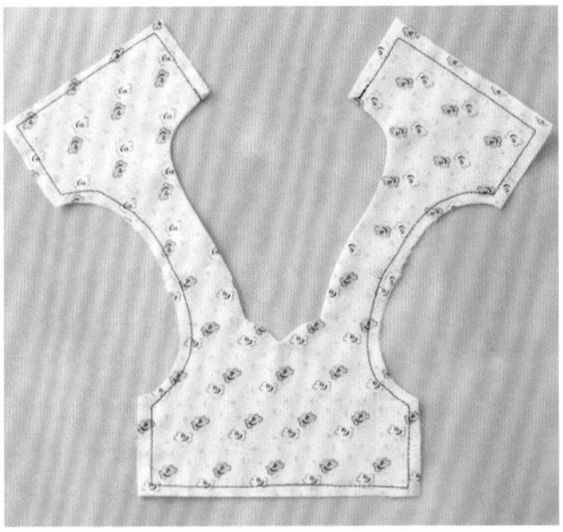

VIEW B

1. Sew the bodice front to the bodice back pieces at the shoulders, right sides together.

2. Press the finished seam allowances toward the back.

3. Make the ruffle piece (see Make a Ruffle, page 18). Pin together, with the wrong side of the ruffle facing the right side of the bodice and the hemmed edge even with the center back raw edge. Sew it to the neckline.

4. Trim the edge of the ruffle even with the angle of the center back edges.

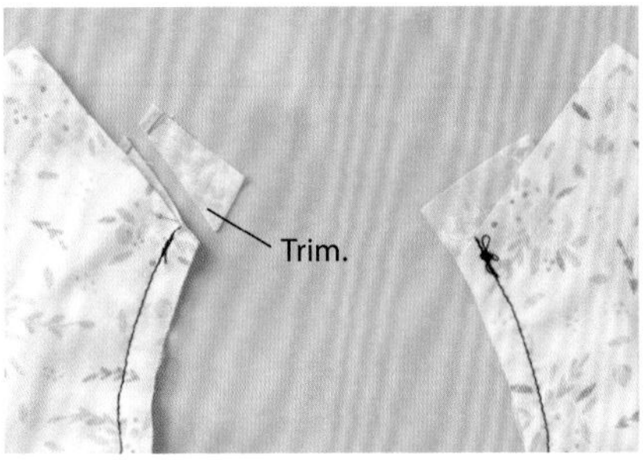

5. Finish the neckline with bias binding (see Finish with Bias Binding, page 11)

Sleeves

VIEW A

Hem the sleeve ends (see Hemming, page 11).

ALL VIEWS

1. Sew gathering stitches along the sleeve caps where indicated on the pattern. Gather the sleeves to fit the bodice.

2. Pin and sew the sleeves to the bodice, right sides together.

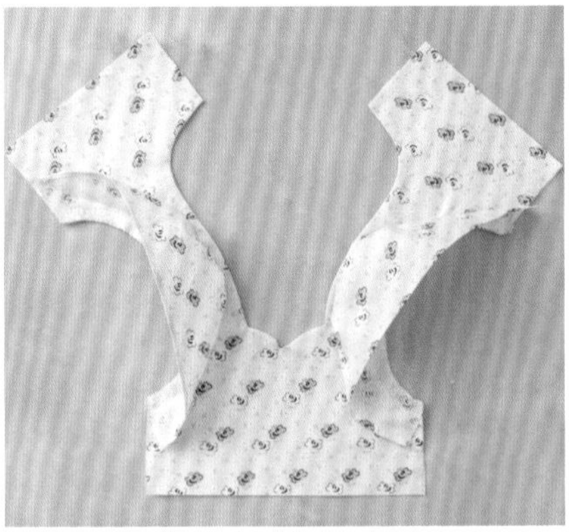

VIEW A

Cut 2 pieces of elastic, each 3½˝ long. Sew the elastic pieces to the wrong side of fabric, ¼˝ from the hemmed edge. Stretch the elastic as you sew (see Elastic Sewn Directly to the Fabric, page 13).

VIEW B

1. Sew gathering stitches along the sleeve ends and gather to fit the bias binding strips.

2. Hem the sleeves with the binding strips (see Finish with Bias Binding, page 11).

Side Seams

ALL VIEWS

Pin and sew the sleeve and side seams with right sides together in one continuous step, keeping the sleeve hems even.

Skirt

VIEW A

Seam Binding Tape Casings

1. *Optional:* Use anti-fray sealant on the ends of the seam binding and allow it to dry. If no anti-fray sealant is used, then fold the raw ends under ½″.

2. From the center of the overskirt piece, measure 3″ to the left of the center on the wrong side of the fabric. Pin and topstitch both pieces of seam binding tape to the wrong side of the overskirt piece, making sure the casings are wide enough for a safety pin.

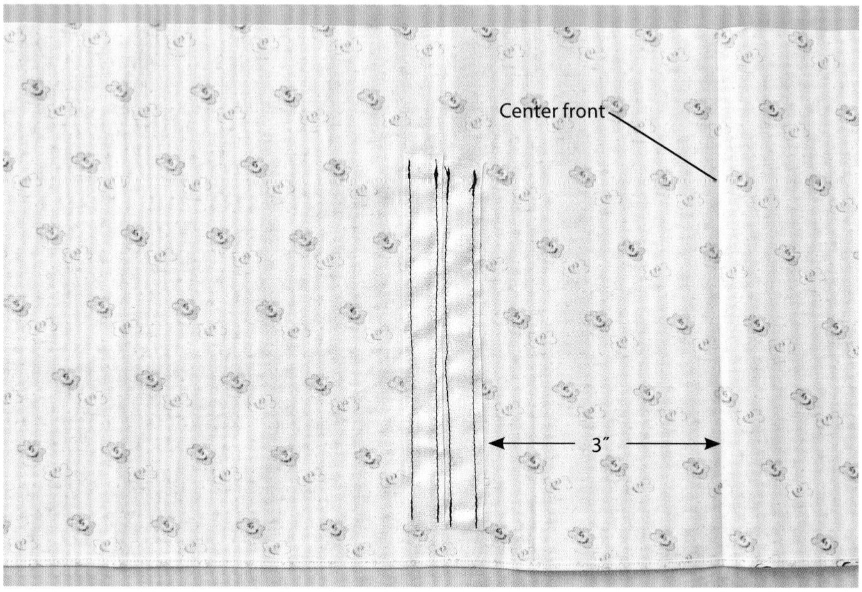

ALL VIEWS

1. Hem the underskirt with lace (see Hemming with Trim, page 12).

2. Sew a narrow hem on the overskirt (see Hemming, page 11).

3. Sew a double-layered skirt to the bodice (see Sew a Double-Layered Skirt, page 16).

Finishing

ALL VIEWS

Sew the center back seam and closure (see Center Back Seam and Closures, page 16).

VIEW A

1. Use a safety pin to feed a piece of ribbon from the hem up into one casing and down out the other casing.

2. Pull both ribbon ends to gather and tie into a bow.

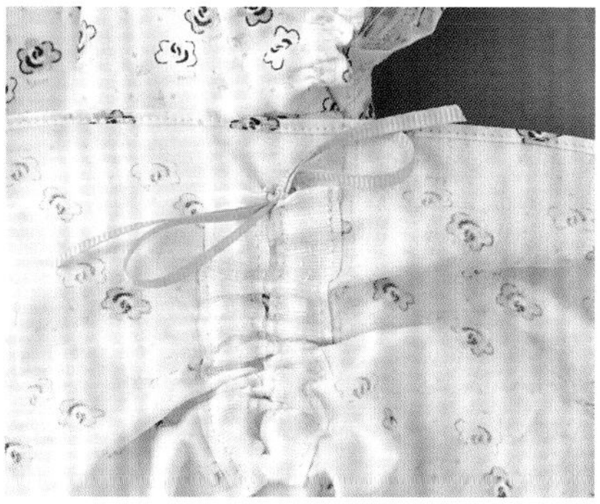

VIEW B

Fold little tucks at the hem; then sew buttons 5″ apart onto the folded fabric to create a scallop-like hem.

Dots and Stripes

Add the sleeves from the Winter Bloom dress (page 57), using the Sleeve 45 pattern. Hem them with lace. Cut the underskirt 8¾˝ × 30˝ and create a plain narrow hem. Add some extra charm and balance to this tea-length design with a gathered sash the same color as the ribbon bows.

Garden Party

Make a quicker version of the Ruffles and Lace dress (page 51). Use lace instead of a ruffle along the neckline, make a shorter single-layer skirt (cut a piece 6˝ × 30˝) hemmed with lace, and add a gathered sash to finish.

CHAPTER SEVEN

Princess-Seamed Dresses

VIEW A: Class Act. **VIEW B:** Blomstring.
VIEW C: Summer Frolic. **VIEW D:** Winter Bloom.

Materials

All views

Lining: 1 fat eighth or ¼ yard

Hook-and-loop tape: ¼ yard

View A

Dress: ⅓ yard

Yoke and contrast hem: ¼ yard

Flat piping: ⅝ yard

Buttons (5⁄16˝ diameter): 4

View B

Center front and back bodice and skirt: 1 fat quarter or ¼ yard of print fabric

Side bodice, yoke, and skirt: 1 fat quarter or ¼ yard of coordinating solid fabric

Belt and bias hem: 2 scraps of coordinating fabrics

Corded piping: 1 yard

Buttons (½˝ diameter): 2

View C

Dress: ⅓ yard

Rickrack trim: 1½ yards

View D

Dress: ½ yard

Collar, flat piping, and sleeve ruffles: 1 fat quarter

Contrast flat piping: 1 fat quarter

Ribbon (⅛˝ wide): ¼ yard

Views A and B have a regular neckline in the back. Views C and D have a slightly scooped neckline in the back.

Cutting

Use the patterns to cut out the fabric pieces (see the pattern pullout for tracing or Patterns, page 7, for downloading and printing instructions). Follow the cutting instructions on the patterns and use a fabric-marking tool to transfer any pattern markings onto the fabric pieces. Use the measurements given below to cut out the remaining pieces needed.

View A

- Bodice Center Front 35, Bodice Center Back A 37, Bodice Side 36, Lining Front 38, Lining Back A 39, and Yoke 40
- Main skirt: 5¾˝ × 30˝
- Contrasting hem: 2½˝ × 30˝
- Flat piping (strips cut on the bias):

  1⅛˝ × 30˝ • 1⅛˝ × 13½˝ • ¾˝ × 5˝

View B

- Bodice Center Front 35, Bodice Center Back A 37, Bodice Side 36, Lining Front 38, Lining Back A 39, Yoke 40, and Belt 41
- Waistband: 1⅜˝ × 12¾˝
- Hem binding: 1½˝ × 31˝
- Skirt:

  Print fabric: 1 piece 6˝ × 6˝ and 2 pieces 3˝ × 6˝

  Solid fabric: 2 pieces 6˝ × 9˝

View C

- Bodice Center Front 35, Bodice Center Back B 42, Bodice Side 36, Lining Front 38, Lining Back B 43, and Flutter Sleeve 44
- Skirt: 6˝ × 30˝

View D

- Bodice Center Front 35, Bodice Center Back B 42, Bodice Side 36, Lining Front 38, Lining Back B 43, Sleeve 45, Skirt Piece 23, and Collar 46
- Sleeve ruffle: 2 pieces 2¼˝ × 10˝
- Narrow flat piping (strips cut on the bias): ¾˝ × 18˝
- Wide flat piping (strips cut on the bias): 1˝ × 18˝

Sewing Instructions

All seams are ¼˝ unless otherwise instructed. Finish and press the seam allowances after sewing each seam.

Flat Piping

VIEWS A AND D

Fold and press the bias strips in half lengthwise with wrong sides together.

Bodice

VIEW B

Pin and sew the piping to the right side of the bodice side pieces. The trim should extend ¼˝ at the top edges.

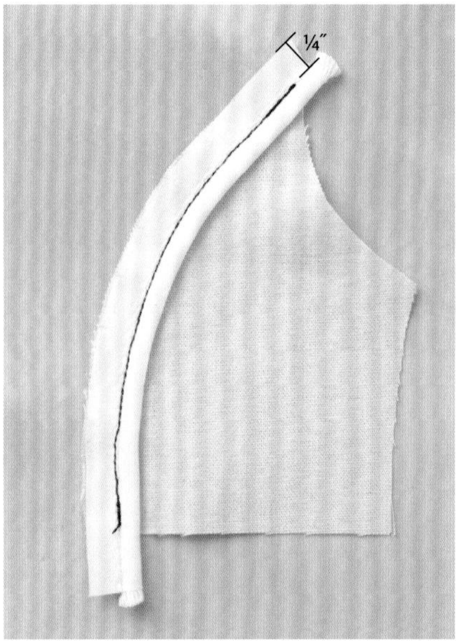

VIEW C

Pin and sew the rickrack to the right side of the bodice center pieces.

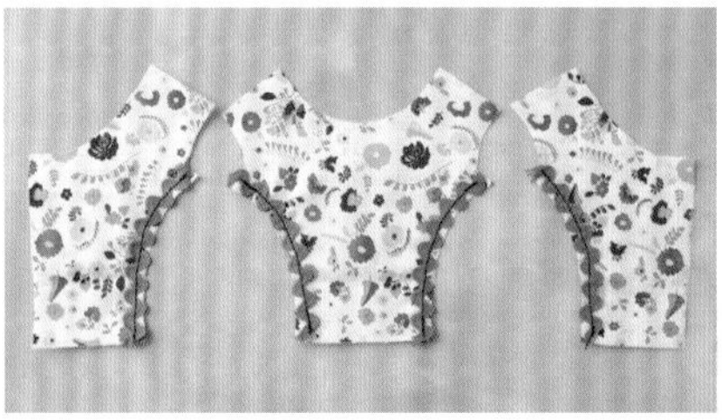

VIEW D

First pin and sew the narrower flat piping pieces to the right side of the bodice side pieces; then add the wider flat piping on top.

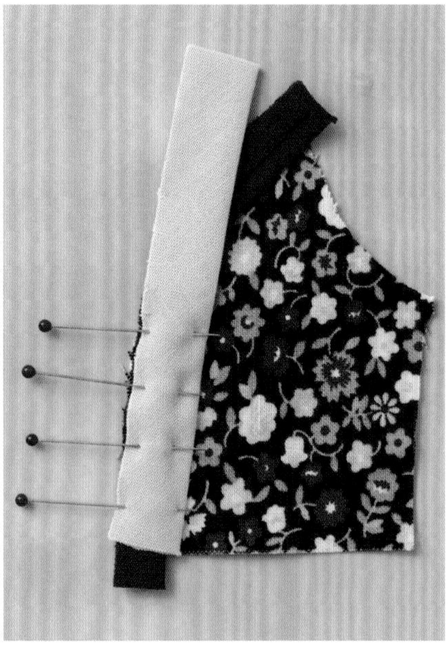

tips

You can add piping to most any seam for an additional design feature that makes a dress, skirt, or top more special. Use simple bias trim (flat piping) as an easier alternative, as in Views A and D.

- *If needed, trim the raw edge of the corded piping so the raw edge measures ¼˝ from the stitching line of the piping.*
- *If necessary, clip within the seam allowance of the piping to make it curve smoothly as you pin together the pieces.*
- *Use a piping presser foot and sew close to the cord. Or use a zipper foot and move the needle position to stitch next to the cord.*

ALL VIEWS

1. Sew the bodice side pieces to the bodice center front piece and the center back pieces, right sides together.

2. Trim the seam allowances using pinking shears or small scissors to cut triangle notches. Press the seam allowances open.

For View C: Don't cut the rickrack trim when trimming the seam allowances; use small scissors and clip only within the gaps.

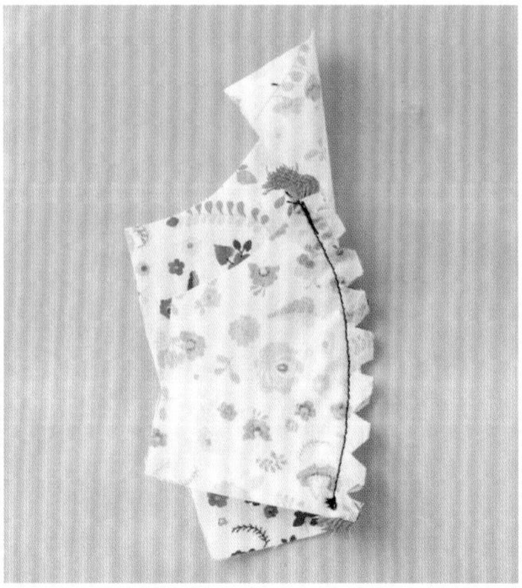

3. For Views B and D: Press the piping/trim towards the bodice center pieces.

For View C: Press the rickrack towards the bodice side pieces.

tips

To ensure correct easing, place pins at the top edge and the bottom edge first; then pin to the center for each princess seam. Make sure not to stretch the fabric when pinning together the pieces.

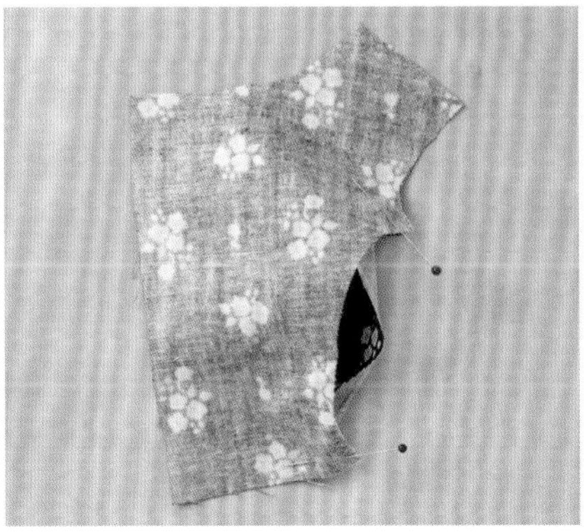

- *Pin and sew with the bodice center pieces facing up. This reduces the chances of sewing a fold into the seam.*
- *If available, use the needle-down feature on your machine.*
- *Sew slowly with a short stitch length (2.0).*
- *Keep the raw edges even the entire length of the seam.*

Yoke

VIEWS A AND B

1. Pin and sew the flat piping or piping to the right side of the lower edge of a yoke piece, keeping the raw edges even.

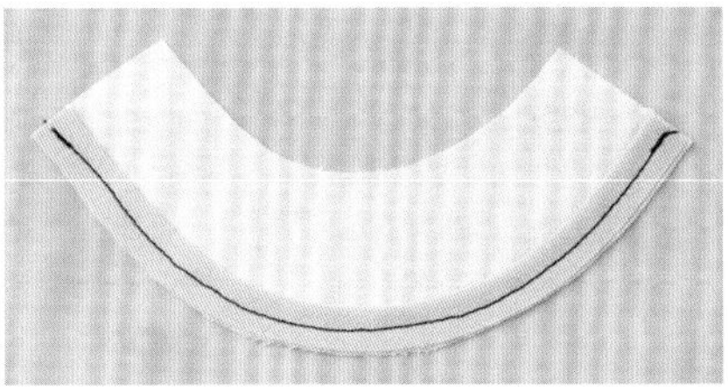

2. Make and sew the yoke piece to the right side of the bodice front at the neckline and the lower edge (see Sew a Collar or Yoke, page 17).

Flutter Sleeves

VIEW C

1. Sew together the sleeve pieces on the curved edge, right sides together.

2. Cut triangle notches within the seam allowances.

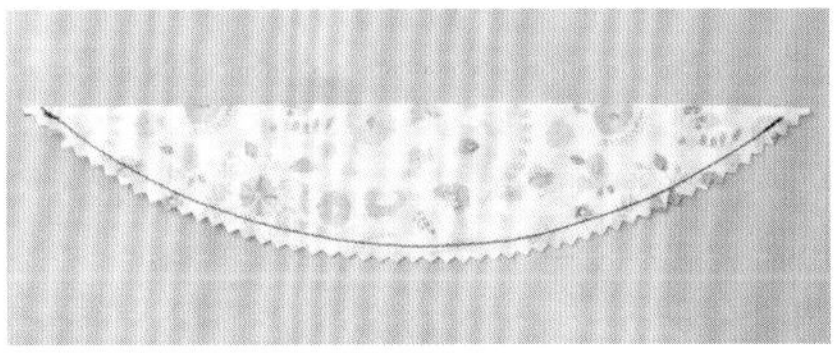

3. Turn the sleeves right side out and press.

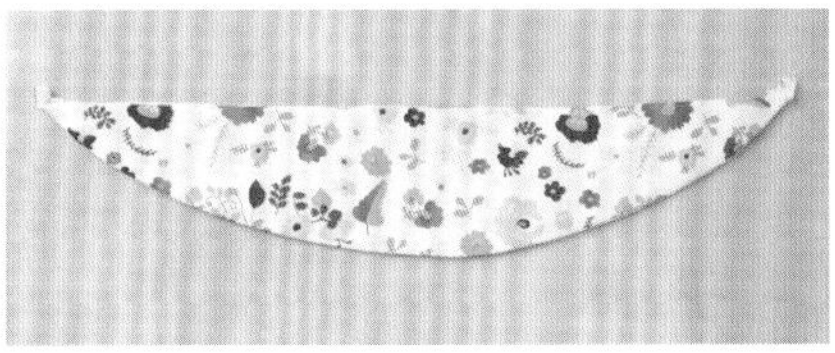

4. Sew gathering stitches along the raw edges and gather to 3¾˝.

Collar

VIEW D

Make the collars (see Sew a Collar or Yoke, page 17).

Sewing the Lined Bodices

VIEWS A AND B

Sew the bodice (see Sew a Lined Bodice Without Sleeves, page 10).

For View A: Pin and sew the flat piping to the right side of the lower edge of the bodice, keeping all the raw edges even.

For View B:

1. Pin and sew the waistband to the bodice, right sides together.

2. Press the finished seam allowances down toward the waistband.

VIEW C

Sew a bodice with flutter sleeves (see Sew a Bodice with Flutter or Half-Cap Sleeves, page 11).

VIEW D

Sew the bodice (see Sew a Lined Bodice with Sleeves, page 9).

Sleeves

VIEW D

1. Fold the ruffle pieces in half lengthwise, wrong sides together, and press.

2. Sew gathering stitches along the raw edges of the ruffle pieces. Gather to fit the sleeve ends.

3. Pin and sew the ruffle to the sleeve ends with right sides together, using a ⅜˝ seam allowance. Topstitch.

4. Sew gathering stitches on the sleeve caps where indicated on the pattern, and gather to fit the arm opening.

5. Pin and sew the sleeves to the bodice with right sides together.

Side Seams

VIEW D

Pin and sew the side and sleeve seams with right sides together in one continuous step, keeping the sleeve hems even.

Skirt

VIEW A

Sew the contrast hem piece with the flat piping to the skirt piece (see Sewing a Contrast Hem, page 12).

VIEW B

Sew the 5 skirt pieces together with right sides together, placing the smaller floral print pieces on the outer edges and the larger floral print piece at the center.

VIEWS A, B, AND C

Sew a gathered skirt to the bodice (see Gathered Skirts, page 14).

For View B: Align the skirt piece with the bodice so that the color-blocked sections match visually.

VIEW D

1. Pin and sew the skirt piece to the bodice with right sides together, using a ⅜″ seam allowance.

2. Press the finished seam allowances toward the bodice.

Belt

VIEW B

1. Make the belt pieces (see Fabric Bow, page 20).

2. Fold and press the raw edges to the inside.

3. Sew the ends of each belt piece to the right side of the bodice, with the belt ends aligned with the princess seams in the back of the dress.

Center Back Opening

ALL VIEWS

Sew the center back seam and closure (see Center Back Seam and Closures, page 16).

Hemming

VIEW B

Hem the dress with bias binding (see Finish with Bias Binding, page 11).

VIEW C

Hem the dress with rickrack trim (see Hemming with Trim, page 12).

VIEW D

Sew a narrow hem (see Hemming, page 11).

Finishing

VIEW A

Sew buttons on the yoke and contrasting hem piece.

VIEW B

Sew buttons on the belt ends on the bodice front.

VIEW D

Make and sew ribbon bows to the sleeves.

Soda Shop

Make the bodice like View A without any piping. If using a directional print, then consider cutting the bodice side pieces on the cross grain. Use the Skirt Piece 23 pattern. Add a bow to the yoke with the Bow 10 pattern. Top it off with a gathered sash (see Make a Fabric Sash, page 17).

Orange Crush

Sew the sleeves and collar from View D, use only one layer of piping, and add the skirt from View C. Hem with lace to complete the look.

Sweeter than Chocolate

Sew the sleeves from the Ruffles and Lace dress (page 51)—from the Sleeves 32 pattern. Make a skirt from the Skirt Piece 23 pattern, hemmed with lace. Finish with a complementary ribbon tied to the waist. *Note:* Use only one layer of flat piping when you are sewing the bodice.

Recital

Use two different solid fabrics and follow the directions for View B, omitting the bodice yoke, piping, and belt. For the skirt, cut and sew together 3 strips 2½˝ × 30˝. To finish, add a classic bow at the center front waist, using the Classic Bow 11 and 12 patterns and following Classic Bow (page 20).

About the Author

ERIN HENTZEL first fell in love with sewing at age seven, when she attended a kids sewing class at the Lucie Stern Community Center in Palo Alto, California. While growing up, she enjoyed sewing stuffed animals for friends and clothing for herself (and, of course, for her dolls!).

Erin earned a bachelor of science degree from Oregon State University and lives in beautiful Willamette Valley, Oregon, with her family, two cats, and a blind chinchilla. She teaches sewing classes locally and runs an Etsy shop, where she sells her Avery Lane sewing patterns.

FOLLOW ERIN ON SOCIAL MEDIA:

Website: averylanesewing.com

Etsy shop: etsy.com/shop/averylane

Facebook: /averylanedesigns

Instagram: @averylanesewing

Avery Lane Patterns Sewing Group: facebook.com > search Avery Lane Patterns Sewing Group

(Join Erin on Facebook to show off your creations, ask sewing questions, join sew-alongs, and enter design challenges!)

Also by Erin Hentzel:

Want even more creative content?
Go to ctpub.com/offer
& sign up to receive our gift to you!
MENU
C&T PUBLISHING
HAND PRINTING STUDIO
Print on Almost Anything!
Get some in-spiration
GET INSPIRED
GARMENT SEWING LOOKBOOK 2016
Make it, snap it, share it
using #ctpublishing